7-FIGURE GODDESS®

MAKING THE LEAP FROM SIX TO SEVEN FIGURES IN TWO YEARS (OR LESS)

ELIZABETH PURVIS

Difference Press

Washington, DC, USA

Published 2022

DISCLAIMERS

Cover Design: Jennifer Stimson

Editing: Natasa Smirnov

Author's photo courtesy of Jessica Daniels

CONTENTS

1. Why You're Working So Damn Hard   1
2. The Truth about You   21
3. The Energy of "Standard"   37
4. The Divine Standard   51
5. The Abundance Standard   75
6. The Confidence Standard   95
7. The Expectation Standard   117
8. The Discipline Standard   137
9. The No Apologies Standard   159
10. The Benevolent Queen Standard   175
11. The Money Impeccability Standard   193
12. The Transformation Standard   215
13. The Energy of Divine Love (The Secret Sauce)   229
14. The Power of Surrender   245
15. Your Seven-Figure Business Is Here Now   255

Acknowledgments   263
About the Author   267
Thank You for Reading   269

To our clients at 7-Figure Goddess®, past present and future…

…and a certain Bright-Arrow-Golden-Girl.

1

WHY YOU'RE WORKING SO
DAMN HARD

Welcome, Leader! I am so very glad you're here.

If you've picked up this book, I'd guess that you might be doing so for a couple of reasons.

One, you're probably a coach, healer, energy worker, conscious expert, or teacher with a big mission. You didn't come here to play small.

Two, you've already created some sweet success – six figures or even multiple six figures in your service-based business.

Three, you want to scale. You're ready for the big leap.

Four, you want it *now*. Like, *now*.

And most of all, you want it to be *easier*.

If we were sitting down together, one-on-one, to talk about your scaling strategy, you might tell me that you're already doing "all the things" to make the income you're making.

"It's good money," you might say, "But I want great money. And I refuse to exhaust myself or compromise my values."

Believe me, I get you. And while the path to seven figures in your coaching, healing, or expert business may never be "easy," it can be much simpler and the journey much faster than you may currently believe.

You're in the right place.

You see, if you were to take a peek at our Facebook Messenger or email inbox – where we do almost all of our enrolling – you'd see things like this:

"My last launch was a disaster. It took two months to prepare, and six weeks to get through. I wanted ten people for my $20k program. I got three."

"For the past three years I've built out this webinar funnel. My traffic costs are huge – $12k per month! That gets me something like twenty sales calls. Two people sign up. I'm just barely breaking even."

"I'm spending literally twenty hours per week on sales calls. I tried to hand it off to a sales team, but it was a disaster. So far, I've gone through nine "sales people" in nine months. I've heard that this is not uncommon."

"I'm already at $250k, but I'm bored. I know I'm supposed to be working with different clients. But I only attract newbies who don't have any money. I can't talk to these people anymore. Help!"

"It took me years to get to where I am now. I don't want it to take years to get to my next income level."

In other words, they *all* say some form of:

"I want things to be easier. I want to collapse time, instead of everything being such a slog."

Maybe you can relate?

Let's face it – this "build a business around your transformation" thing isn't easy.

Getting a business off the ground is hard. You've got to figure out what the heck you're offering, and why anyone would care, let alone pay you. Picking a niche, attracting those first prospects, having those first sales conversations, saying your fee for the first time (without wanting to throw up) – none of it was easy, was it?

Growing a business to that first six figures or multi-six figures is also hard – the cycle of marketing for clients, getting the clients, delivering to those clients, staying up late to get emails or an opt-in page done for your launch, working through the weekends, hiring that first virtual assistant or "techie" to get everything set up, managing that person, resisting the temptation to do everything yourself!

And – of course! – then comes wondering where the heck all the money goes the second you make it. (Turns out, $100,000 or even $200,000 in annual income doesn't go very far.)

I remember the day I left my last j-o-b. My dad – who moonlighted as a highly paid consultant when he wasn't teaching at our local university – tried to warn me about the challenges ahead.

I remember shrugging him off in an email. *How hard can it be?* I thought, as I typed out my response. ("I'm fine, it'll be fine…")

'Tis to laugh!

Not everyone can run their own business, delivering their knowledge, service, or expertise. We think, *If I could just get to that first $10k per month. Or – gasp - $20k. Everything would be amazing!*

But then, as we evolve, a different kind of "hard" emerges.

When we start in business, we get to learn all of the things about running a business. Who are you serving? How do you help them? How can you package up what you do or know, so you can serve them well?

We get through those first enrollment convos. We learn how to receive money without wanting to throw up.

We get to that $100k finish line or even that $200k.

And then, the truth about the game becomes clear.

If we want to do this thing called "make a ton of money and have a great lifestyle while delivering our most important work in the world" (what I like to call your Highest Level Transformation), and do it long term, and maybe even build wealth doing it, then those first six figures or multi-six figures aren't, in fact, the endgame.

That's the starting line.

That's where the journey *begins* rather than ends.

Years ago, when I began mentoring transformational leaders (who I will refer to as "Leaders," throughout this book) in that $100k to $200k income range, I had just come off years of mentoring "newbie" business owners: new coaches, therapists, and even a rocket scientist or two leaving their practices to start their businesses.

In the "newbie" stage of business, there's just one goal: figure out how to make enough money to not go back to a day job!

When those clients would reach that "$10k per month" goal and then come into our mastermind, they were excited. Time to scale!

In short order, though, that excitement would turn to terror.

"Wait a minute. You mean, now, it's time to actually do this business thing?"

Hilariously, the name of our program was the Desire Mastermind.

It's not easy following the Desires of your heart.

IT'S NOT YOUR STRATEGY

When you're in the throes of working ten hours every weekend, or you snapped at your kids or your spouse or your dog because you just spent six hours messing with your website yourself (you hired someone to do it, but dang it all, they're *just not getting it*) …

Or you want to sign up ten people this month, but *none* of your well-crafted "authority" posts or high-end branding photos are getting any traction online …

Well, it's easy to look to strategy.

After all, once you've decided to increase your numbers and make more income, the "doing" never stops.

Sales calls. Webinars. Opt-in pages for said webinar. Automated email sequences. Podcast or YouTube? Hang on – the woman who apparently has a nine-figure coaching empire says you need publicity, now, too? Facebook is looking lamer by the day, so you've been messing around with LinkedIn. Now you're filtering through three cold pitches from complete strangers a day.

Fix the website, it's outdated again. And the myriad – myriad! – emails and social media posts, just to be seen amid countless souls with seemingly louder megaphones.

Not to mention the sales calls. Only now they're in Messenger and Insta DMs. It's called "social selling," right?

Yep – all that marketing strategy is a *lot* of work. But there's something you may not have noticed along the way.

For your consideration, let's examine one possible "week in the life" of one on our clients. I'll call her Lisa.

What I'm about to share *might* sound familiar. It's a common picture among our clients.

Lisa "arrives" at her desk on a Monday morning and sits down to dive into her day. First thing, she checks Slack.

There's a note from her business manager: "Don't look at the email from Julie!"

That's kinda like saying "Don't think of a gray elephant," so, of course she looks.

The words cut deep.

"I don't think this program is working for me…"

"Been in for two months and something is off…"

"I gave it a good try, but it's not aligned…"

Lisa's head starts spinning. She counts up the numbers.

If she asks for a refund, I'm going to end up short for the month.

She keeps reading.

"Too many promises…"

"It's not in integrity…"

Of course, this means that she's going to have to have one of *those* conversations. Lisa hired her new business manager to have *those* conversations. But with all that has been going on, she just hasn't had time to train her properly.

Wait a minute. Are my claims out of integrity? Are they

even legal? I have to get a lawyer, now? Shit. Lisa's mind is inundated with worst-case scenarios.

Lisa looks up and a *half hour* has gone by.

Lisa's phone beeps. It's one of her private clients. The client is upset. Clearly stressed. A thing happened. And when Lisa reads between the lines... *Hang on... is she... kinda blaming me for this?*

Lisa needs to prepare for her call in an hour. But after all the stimuli, her brain begs for a numb-out. So, she finds herself on Instagram, scrolling ... scrolling ... scrolling ... .

Lisa sees a post from her business bestie. Said bestie is celebrating a $300,000 launch. Of course, Lisa is *happy* for her, of course....

Of course.

Next thing you know, Lisa peeps the clock. Just fifteen minutes before she has to get on to lead her mastermind call....

Personally, my energy tanks when I read that. (Especially since I've lived scenes like this many times!)

Heck, my energy tanked as I wrote that!

When I read that, it feels ... hard.

And yet, did you notice something?

There are very few "to-dos" happening here.

In fact, there's very little going down externally at all.

Lisa "got to work." There was an email.

The only "to-do" on the list was to prepare for the call.

And yet, by high noon in these kinds of days, well, it's exhausting, is it not?

And that's the thing.

When we realllly slow down and pay attention to what's really going on in our business, we might – might! – notice that the *real* cause of "working hard" is rarely what's on our list for the day.

What makes things feel hard is our *reaction* to what's on the list and our reaction to whatever decision, problem, fire to fight, or *shitburger* (yes, this is an actual term) happens to fly into our field in the normal course of doing business.

Let's say you decide you're going to hire a new contractor to take care of some lame-o marketing tasks – your seven postings a day on social or whatever. It's not getting done. OK, so maybe seven posts is overkill. But, you know you have to do at least *one* per day. (You actually don't, but that's another story for another time.)

Lisa also has to hire. But man, does hiring stress her out. *The position needs a unicorn. Damnit, I'll never find a unicorn.* Besides, the last supposed-unicorn ended up posting pictures of Lisa's kids in the bathtub on Instagram (!) – the fire in the comments section was off the chain.

See? Nobody can do this stuff as well as I can, Lisa justifies her reluctance to herself.

So Lisa does what's only natural in this situation. She procrastinates. Meanwhile, the job continues to not get done by her. She feels guilty, on top of all the despair that she'll never find anyone good.

If I can't find someone good for my fricking Instagram account, how am I supposed to find a business manager?

This kind of self-talk happens in an instant, by the way. You barely even notice it, but it's there. And in that fail to notice, you *also* fail to notice that it's really, really weighing on you.

Now, sure, if you're Lisa, you've gotta hire the person. Eventually you'll heave a heavy sigh and hire someone. You'll make with the logistics.

But the logistics *aren't hard.*

What's *hard,* and what makes things *feel hard* is waiting a year before you finally just give in and just effing do it.

What's *hard,* and what makes things *feel hard* is rarely the "thing" itself.

What's *hard,* and what makes things *feel hard* is our *response* to the "thing" – our projecting "what if?" into the future or remembering what happened the last time the team dropped the ball or the client backed out or whatever.

The story we attach to "the thing" is what makes it hard.

What's *hard* and what makes things *feel hard* is our resistance.

THE REAL CAUSE OF WORKING HARD: INNER FRICTION

Inner Friction: n. the emotional response that occurs – from slight tension to full on trigger-induced meltdown – from a belief or story about a situation.

"What if she ends up backing out?"

"What if it doesn't work?"

"I don't want to look like an idiot…"

Whatifwhatifwhatif….

And it makes everything feel *hard*.

Getting "The Email" feels *hard*. Finding "The Unicorn" feels *hard*.

Watching days go by and the social media posts don't get done and every day you're reminded of how it's not getting done, and then, oh, boy, look at that, your bestie just made $300,000 feels hard.

And it's everywhere. Indeed, if you're at six figures in your business, and you're actually *in* there "doing the do," so to speak – you're doing the work, showing up, doing your best to get clients and moving forward in spite of whatever is thrown at you that day, inner friction is something you're experiencing on, well, pretty much a daily basis.

Our days feel *hard*, instead of the ease, grace, freedom, flow, and *lightness* we long for.

Another reason why it's hard is because your emotions are a biological as well as an emotional process. When you're feeling stressed, let's say, your body has to load up a bunch of instructions and fire off a whole host of steps and chemicals to "do stress." It adds energy and calories to an already very full day. And it seems like you're doing so damn much, when you know so much of your time is going to fighting fires or feeling the feels.

Inner friction robs you of time and focus. All those hours you spend pouring into the worries, fears, reactions, "will they or won't they," or "can I or can't I" is time you'll never get back.

Inner friction is real. When you're at that six-figure or multi-six-figure mark, you might not realize how much space it's taking up.

Nonetheless, there's another reason why stressful emotions and inner friction are problems. They directly impact your ability to create and what you *do* create.

A CRASH COURSE IN HOW YOU CREATE YOUR REALITY (OR, INNER FRICTION STRIKES AGAIN)

What I'm about to share is at the heart of your ability to collapse time – that is, go from six figures to seven figures in two years or less and have it be (relatively!) smooth and joyful, a path of ease and speed, instead of years of slog, bumping up against your income ceiling.

At the heart of *that* (your ability to collapse time)

is Universal Law – which you'll also hear me describe as the Law, the Laws, or just Law, as in "by Law."

If you've read *Think and Grow Rich* or *The Science of Getting Rich*, you've had exposure to the Law. (*The Secret* is debatable, but at least it put Law on the map again.)

The Law is, in Wallace Wattles's words, "the uniform and orderly method of the omnipotent God."

Is the Law "real"? The mainstream loves to debate this.

Personally, I'm not here for debate. Since I was a "wee witchlet" running around New York City in my early twenties learning magic, my goal has been: *discover what works.*

After many, many years of study and practice, I have come to know that the Law is the *spiritual* capital-T Truth about the way the world works. The spiritual and metaphysical foundations of how we create our reality. It starts with what I refer to as Frequency, or vibration. What I will also refer to as your "vibrational signature."

Frequency is the vibration, or the energy pattern, that is given off by your way of being. In practice, it's who you *be*. How are you showing up. A combo platter of your thoughts, your emotions, your physical being, and, of course, the actions that you take. Taken together, all of those things make up your Frequency, or vibrational signature. You "broadcast" your Frequency constantly, into the field of energy that surrounds us.

Everything is made up of *energy*. And that energy is *not* static – it vibrates. William Walker Atkinson's *The Kybalio*n, one of the best- known books about Universal Law, calls this the Law of Vibration. "Everything vibrates, nothing rests."

We are energy, and of course, we are surrounded by a field of energy – Creative Substance, Creative Life Force energy, God/Goddess, Source, Spirit, or just the Field, as I'll refer to it. We are *of* it, and we live *in* it. We couldn't get away from it if we tried.

All physical and mental (metaphysical) science is based on the First Law, that this energy – the Field – "just is." And that it is always moving from a non-form, into a form, and back again. This is the Law of Perpetual Transmutation.

And you're "impressing the Field" all day every day with your way of *be*-ing.

Why does that matter? Because it responds to us. This vast *sea* of energy that we all come from, and swim in, is constantly responding to us. And it responds to us in the only way it can, which is by feeding you back exactly the same Frequency as your own. It operates completely deductively. It *can't* give us back anything other than what we put in.

The Field functions by receiving input from us in the form of frequency and giving us that input back. This is why you hear manifestation teachers talk about attracting things that are your energetic match. What's interesting, though, is that it happens on the level of *thought*.

If you want a Tesla, say, you don't become the vibration of the Tesla and then the Tesla vibrates into your living room. That does *not* happen.

When you become that Frequency match - and you send out *thoughts* of a certain vibration – the Field *must*, by Law, respond in kind.

How does it respond? By bringing things into your awareness. Perceptions. Opportunities. Things "showing up." Things you can see.

One of the most important things to know, and remember, about manifestation is that it's *not* about creating "stuff" out of thin air. Manifesting is about becoming aware – or being able to perceive – things that *already exist* in your environment.

You impress the Field with your Frequency, and you perceive (and attract) in kind. What you experience on the "3D" plane is directly related to how you're showing up – how you're BE-ing.

So, when you're triggered, or stressed, or full of Inner Friction, of course this affects your vibration. Not only is it hard to take action, and not only is all of your energy going into *a black hole*, but you're going to miss the opportunities and perceptions for it to be easy. (Or easier, at least.)

When our clients come to us and say, "I want to stop working so hard. I want to collapse time. I want it to be *easy*" – they know there's no "easy" Button. They're not afraid of hard work.

Like you, they want it to be easier!

What they're really craving is flow. Flow happens in the absence of friction. Friction disappears when all parts of you are aligned. When there's no inner static or inner conflict.

THE "HIGHER PERFORMER PARADOX"

It's kind of funny, the crazy paradoxes that high-performing women have been conditioned to live with and tolerate.

High-performers, those of us who are proudly "type A," get things *done*. Most of us create more miracles and results in a month than a good chunk of the population does in six months to a year. And yet, high-performing women are the ones most likely to think they're not doing enough.

High-performing women do great things. Our projects are big and bold. We tackle the kinds of problems that make a difference. We're willing to go where many people simply won't – and that includes those dark corners of the psyche that drive disempowering behaviors. So, we can integrate and step into the light.

And yet, high-performing women *deny* their greatness. We know we're great, but ... we have *sooo* many ways we're not perfect – the credit card debt, the fifth failed long-term relationship, the coming in eleventh in the class, the "trying hard" to bust through the $100k to $250k ceiling.

Oh, this old thing? Oh, who me? You must have me confused with someone else.

We have big Desires (with a capital "D"), to be sure. We want a *lot*.

And yet, high-performing women *deny* what they really want . Taking the same clients, year after year, when they know they're meant to work with the best of the best, giving up the vacation again, looking around and convincing themselves that they're just fine, right here where they are – w hen all they really want to do is drop the drama, make the damn money, and get on with it.

90 PERCENT ENERGY, 10 PERCENT EXECUTION

You've heard of the eighty-twenty rule, yeah?

The Pareto Principle was popularized by Tim Ferriss. Eighty percent of your results come from just 20 percent of your inputs.

At 7-Figure Goddess®, we've noticed that up to 90 percent of your results come from your energy, or what Frequency you're rocking, and just 10 percent from execution.

What does this mean?

Ninety percent of your results ultimately come

from how you show up. Who you *be* is the most important element rather than the specifics of what you do.

Of course, that 10 percent execution is crucial. When clients come to us wanting to scale their transformational service business or expert business, we do the deep dive with them. We make sure they have the offers and messaging that speak directly to their Next Level clients and that can, ultimately, propel them to the income level they choose.

The only way that people can say yes to your work is if they can see and understand that you have the right solution to the right person at the right time – that is, your offer. When the way you package your magic is *not* optimized, you're going to be right back on that hustle train. And indeed, that's what many Leaders find themselves doing.

Of course, there are so many more parts to "10 percent execution." But here's the mystical bit about *what* to execute – a.k.a. "the How."

Ultimately, there are a zillion ways to get to your goal. If you want to make seven figures, there are literally hundreds, if not thousands, of possible ways to get there. Similarly, in the online space, there are dozens of ways to scale. Some of these have become popular *not* because they are the "best," but because they solve the problem, and their creators had a bigger bullhorn. In other words, they were committed to getting their way out there.

But no matter what "execution" bits are required for you, or what you are choosing, if your energy *isn't* there, it's going to be a lot harder. You have to be in energetic alignment with what you say you want.

The "mechanics of manifestation" won't bring you those right opportunities. You won't see the right clients. You won't attract the required awareness to get you there.

More importantly, though, good old inner friction will be stopping you at every turn.

In other words, you're gonna be working so damn hard.

SOMETHING "MORE INTERESTING"?

Several years ago, I heard two of the personal growth greats, Cynthia Kersey of the Unstoppable Foundation and her mentor Bob Proctor, hosting a call together.

They were swapping stories of how they met and the early days of their friendship. Then Cynthia told a story of a "Bob Truthbomb."

It was a rough time for Cynthia. After many years of marriage, and years of "trying," Cynthia was staring divorce smack in the face. It wasn't a matter of if, but when.

Sitting together at a meal, Cynthia shared her fears about getting back on her feet. She talked about it being rough and taking months of therapy.

Bob sat there quietly, taking it all in. Finally, he spoke.

"Well," he said simply. "You could do that. The months of therapy."

"Or, you could do something more interesting."

Bob's comment wasn't meant to be flippant or dismissive of the pain Cynthia was in. It was just presenting another option.

Most of the time, when we are "in it" in our businesses – when we're all up in the friction and the emotion – we don't realize how much time it's really taking or how much it's really costing us. What's more, when faced with a problem, our human mind wants us to focus on *one*.

We don't realize there are options. We can't *see* the other possibilities that are right in front of us, waiting to be accessed.

We can keep spinning our wheels, following the hustle train, keep "trying" to scale past that initial multi-six figures of success, or we can skip the friction and just *do* the thing.

We can do something more interesting.

2

THE TRUTH ABOUT YOU

We all are called in different ways. Personally, I got my marching orders from the Goddess on an unassuming day in March 2009, in Prospect Park, Brooklyn.

By that time, I had been working for myself for just over two years. While I'd had my first big "manifesting win" a couple of months before, I was still completely broke. Because two years in, it was only at that point that I'd started to get a teeny bit of a clue about how to get clients and make money.

It wasn't pretty. My days were spent in a constant state of anxiety and fear; my mind was racing with thoughts of "who the f**k are you" and "why on *earth* did you think you could do this?!"

Before that, I'd spent about a decade as an engineer, building computer networks for startups in Silicon Alley in New York. When I wasn't getting up at two in the morning to fix broken servers or wiring up new fleets of servers to deliver web pages twenty-four / seven (also at two in the morning), I was running around New York City, attending rituals and learning magic.

I was already thinking about a "career change," of sorts, by the time the Goddess got to me. A few years previous, I realized that I was meant to create a lot more than just computer networks, and *of course*, I've known that since I was maybe six years old. I'd gotten in deep with New York's rich and colorful comics industry scene and various groups of sci-fi / fantasy authors who called the city home base.

I wanna be a writer, I thought.

And so, when I finally quit my j-o-b as an engineer, I thought it was to write books and comics. But I got a gig writing *sales letters*, of all things. The long-form advertisements I'd get tucked in between the electric bill and that subscription to *New York Magazine*, purchased by my mother.

That gig will make the money, I thought, *while I spend my days doing, you know, the real work.*

Instead, I found that I kind of *liked* writing the "sleazy" sales letters that made money. And I did more digging into what was to become the "online coaching space."

Wait a second. You mean I can make my own thing and sell it this way? All I've gotta do is send some emails and peeps can buy my stuff? Where do I sign?!

From there, I found myself in one hell of an identity crisis. I'd poured *so* much into "being a writer" and had dozens if not at least a hundred friends who were actually established, working, known writers ("famous"). Naturally, discovering that I actually liked this crazy thing called direct response marketing even *more* than the original plan was a kick in the face.

I was supposed to be this writer and live this creative life and now I'm selling eBooks on eBay and writing letters to sell crystal merkabas *via the mail?*

It was bad, especially because I actually *liked* writing "the crystal *merkaba*" letters. I'd seen the power of it.

For two years, I was in a state of paralysis. And despite all my "witch cred" and studying magic for well over a decade, and despite getting good at meditating, directing energy, and "controlling my ego," I found myself *woefully* unequipped to deal with the realities of said ego's daily *screams* over not having enough money and living on credit cards.

The *littlest* things could take me out for days. I spent half the time walking around triggered and the other half depressed, a feeling of malaise hanging over me like a wet blanket.

I was focused on service, though. So, I started working with some Tarot readers to help them get more business. Several of them went from $1,000 months to $5,000 months in very short order. The fact that I, myself, was only making $1,000 per month didn't seem to matter.

So, by the time I got to that fateful day in March, it was bad.

Luckily, there was a lot I could lose myself in. Every day, I would walk from our apartment right around the corner from Greenwood Cemetery on 20th Street to Prospect Park, where I would walk the loop, plotting and scheming, and "what will people think of me-ing" all day long.

Until one day, while I was walking in the park, She spoke:

"You are here to be a part of the movement to bring magic to the mainstream. You'll write books, and you'll put magic in the books. You are here to be a teacher of magic to those who would not otherwise see."

My response?

What?

Are you kidding me right now….

Then, I broke down crying.

No … no, Lady. You're confused. In case you haven't noticed, I literally can't manifest my way out of a paper bag.

I'm broke. We have been living off credit cards.

There's no way. No way.

"There is a way," she said. "You'll find your way."

Oh, Goddess, you have me confused with someone else.

Oh, Goddess,

She said, "Sister.

"Sister....

"Remember who you Are."

THE TRUTH ABOUT YOU

So, let's get right into it.

There's a Truth about you. One that you probably don't yet know. Indeed, we spend most of our lives alternatively blissfully unaware of this Truth or trying to hide from it.

In fairness, for almost all of time, the Truth has been "out there," it has only been given to a select few. (Kinda like *The Secret*. Only not because it was actually a secret.)

Those people were initiates, having to devote themselves to a mystery school for at least five years before it was revealed to them or equivalent in other magical traditions.

We don't have that kind of time, so I'm just going to have it out with you.

Here goes:

You are Divine. The Divine is You.

Or, as we say in my tradition:

Thou art Goddess.

You are Divine. *You* are made up of the same energy as the Divine; you are Divine.

You are not separate from it, you are *it*.

Your Highest Level (as we say in 7-Figure Goddess®) is Thou Art Goddess. Your Highest Level is the awareness of, and energetic alignment with, this Divine Aspect.

We call this the Divine Standard. We're going to deep dive on it very shortly and return to it for the rest of the book.

It's the bottom line, though, so I'm giving it to you right up front.

It doesn't feel true. When your third client has emailed to drop out of your program – it doesn't feel true. When you hit your $10k or $20k income plateau *again* for the month, despite pouring all your energy into a huge launch, it doesn't feel true.

Nonetheless, it is very true.

It was always true about you. It will *always* be true about you.

And that truth is that Thou Art Goddess. You are a Divine Being and all of the implications that naturally follow from this one Truth.

In Feminine Magic® we talk about what I call the two halves of the manifesting equation (I'll break this down later in the book). The first is this truth. Thou Art Goddess. You are like God, you are God-like. Because you and God/dess are of the same substance.

No, your printer is not God, even though it is also of the same substance. Because your printer doesn't have the creative faculties that you have: will, imagination, intellect, and the power to choose.

This might fly in the face of some of your religious beliefs and that's not what I am trying to do here.

Take a deep breath. If you need to put this book down and move on to something else, I'll totally understand.

My point is, you have massive, massive powers of creation, given to you by the Divine, from whom you are *not* separate.

You have creative power. You are not separate from Life but are a part of *it*. You contribute to it, and it contributes to you.

Making this shift into the awareness – the deep, *deep* awareness that Thou Art Goddess and, therefore, are *more* than your thoughts, feelings, and 3D experience – is the very first shift and, in some ways, the *only* shift you need to make. Everything else we do from an energetic standpoint – everything you will read in this book - is about cultivating this awareness within yourself and making it part of your Frequency – your energy pattern that communicates with Creative Substance.

When the Inner Friction is on *high*, jacked up on emotions, the *brain* (who, in our company, we affectionately call "Brian") shuts down linear, rational thinking. I probably don't need to tell you that Brian – a.k.a. your *brain* – is telling you lies. You're an entrepreneur, after all!

What I *can* tell you – the thing I didn't know that day in Prospect Park but did discover, and have spent many, many years working on – is that the faster we step out of those lies and step into this *aligned* Truth and hold it in our conscious awareness and take action from *that* place, the faster you will move.

The leaps will come faster. Six figures to seven can happen in two years or less.

It can happen in a heartbeat, if you let it, because it's *here now*.

SHUTTING IT ALL DOWN

After I got my marching orders, I got to work. I became one of the first teachers of the high-end model in the online coaching industry. I worked with women entrepreneurs, helping them to charge higher fees. I mentored my first client to her first $100k program sale in 2011. (She was, and still is, a channel, by the way. You know, in case you think you can't charge $100k unless you "help people make money.")

I honed my metaphysical chops. I got better at magic. I taught magic to my clients, both in and out of their business programs, so they could have easy access to the potent toolkit that is magic to make their next leaps.

I built one of the first mentoring programs teaching conscious women entrepreneurs how to create, market, and fill high-end programs. I sold it to thousands of people. I created *tons* of competitors along the way, in all kinds of industries.

Everyone was learning from me because – frankly – I'd figured it out.

I also built one of the first twelve-month coaching programs for new entrepreneurs to help them get to their first six figures. Between these two offerings, I sailed to high multi-six and then seven figures and stayed there for many years.

I loved it – until I didn't.

I loved it, until I was miserable with the launching, the constant marketing, the hustle, and that nagging feeling that I wasn't yet doing my *real* work in the world.

I loved high-end, but the way I was teaching it felt like a straitjacket. I felt like I couldn't work with who I *really* wanted to work with or say what I really wanted to say. *What if everyone leaves? If I do it the way I really want to do it, will anyone actually show up?*

Inner Friction was once again all over the place. I was bored as all get-out. I wanted to shut everything in my business down, but I didn't feel like I could. *This is a seven-figure business*, I thought. *I can't just shut it all down. What if I never have anything else to offer?*

I shut it down – seven-figure business one day, zero new income coming in the next. With *me* as the primary breadwinner.

Lemme tell ya – there is *nothing* like being the one responsible for the bills getting paid and to have *no* income coming in. The amount of emotional drama is off the chicken.

Little did I know that the Standards, the system of collapsing time that you're about to learn, was born in those moments. Because I started leaning on that Truth about Me, the Truth that my teachers taught me, the Truth that She wouldn't let me forget.

Thou art Goddess, Goddess. So, how about this …

This problem right here? This client/vendor/online mean girl in your face, this mentor who said she loves you but is really a bully?

This problem. This one right here …

What would happen if you approached this as you approach your magic?

What if this moment is the time for your Divine Self to come out? What if this moment was the moment that you saw the Divine… in them?

What would a 7-Figure Goddess do?

The more I asked that question, the easier it was to sail through the friction, like I had a sail at my back.

Not all of the time, mind you. The perception of "Thou Art Goddess" is just that – a perception. Underneath our perceptions, we have coded behaviors and ingrained reactions, core wounds, and deep gashes. Lies that are so deep, Brian and the body take them on autopilot, because they are "safe" to Brian and the body.

Sometimes, you've got to bust through those blocks. I did a lot of inner work and subconscious reprogramming and repatterning along the way.

The conscious awareness of "Thou Art Goddess," though, was an awareness of the Truth.

"There has to be a way to do this business my way," I said. "There has to be a way for me to teach high-end that is meaningful for me, in integrity for me. My way. And it has to be already here, because the Law says that any and every Desire we have is already Here Now."

And sure enough, it was.

When "my way" dropped in, it came in hot. And I pushed aside *everything* else I was doing to stay afloat while awaiting the instructions from Goddess.

Activate the energy of Confidence. Activate the energy of Expectation. Activate the energy of Discipline.

Divine Love is the Secret Sauce.

No Apologies, Goddess. Be the Benevolent Queen.

A little over a year later, I was back to seven figures in sales.

THE VERSION OF YOU WHO ALREADY HAS IT

In Feminine Magic®, which is my brand name for my metaphysical teachings, we work with Frequency and vibration by connecting with mental creations, or thought forms, that we create in the non-physical realms.

You've likely heard the line from Mike Dooley: "Thoughts are things."

Magicians know that thoughts absolutely *are* things and that every human is already a master at manifesting. We create in the non-physical realms instantly, through imagination.

Magicians also know that in the non-physical realms, there are literally infinite possibilities that already exist. So even though you might be feeling a lot of "hard" in your business right now, somewhere out there in the spirit realm is a version of you that already exists that has your business exactly as you want it. The business, the clients, the money, the experiences you're longing for.

Just as there is a Truth about you, this is a spiritual Truth about your business.

Your seven-figure business, or high-multi-six, or $500k with three months off a year, or whatever it is, it already *exists*.

It's already here.

It is a Desire of your Heart. You've fed it with your imagination, which means that by *Law*, it is already here. (This is the Law of Polarity, which I'll break down a little later on.)

And it's exactly as you want it because you get to have it how you want it.

And there are things standing in the way.

That Inner Friction that affects us, which keeps us from seeing, being in, and fully embodying our Divine Nature, throws up roadblocks and mirages in your business. You literally cannot perceive the opportunities that already exist to manifest those

Desires quickly. Instead, your mind perceives challenges – what you do *not* have.

When you embody the expression of your Divine Nature that is a vibrational match for your Desires – a high-multi-six- or seven-figure business, in this case – you impress the Field with *that* vibration. By Law, the Field can *only* give back to you opportunities and perceptions that are in alignment with that vibration.

Collapsing time in your business, then, looks something like this:

One, align with Truth. (Spiritual Truth. Universal Law. Your Divine Nature.)

Two, eliminate the Inner Friction.

When you do this, you'll receive the Way. ("The Way" is the *how*: the specific moves for your visions, dreams, and Desires to become real.)

Take the actions shown to you from the place of your Divine Nature. Your 7-Figure Goddess®.

Your seven-figure business will become real.

WE BELIEVE

It has been well over a decade since the Goddess gave me my marching orders and that loving kick in the pants.

Back in those days, those of us in the transformation industry knew we were at the forefront of something big.

"Consciousness is speeding up," we'd say. "The old structures and barriers are crumbling down. They can no longer stand." We'd pour these words and that sentiment into our content and sales letters.

Being there back then, I had the distinct feeling that we could all sense something, but we didn't *quite* know what we were talking about.

Now, we know.

Consciousness is speeding up. The old structures and barriers are crumbling down. They can no longer stand. The entire world is in the middle of a major turning point.

Which is why the magicians are rising. And why being a part of the movement to bring magic – that is, transformational work – to the mainstream has been our mission at 7-Figure Goddess®, since the day that She shared it with me.

By *you* doing *your* work – and people *want* your work, they want it more than you know – we truly usher in the consciousness that we all say that we want.

This is why I believe that magicians should be paid as much as doctors.

If you're reading this, I see you.

You're not here to hang out at six figures for the rest of your professional life.

You are here to do something significant.

You are here, in no small part, to do your part in

bringing magic to the mainstream. And to make an extraordinary living doing it.

Which means the time for you to *live* into your greatness is now. The time to release the Inner Friction and embody your Highest Level – your Divine Nature – your 7-Figure Goddess® is now.

The time to make the leap to seven figures is now. Ninety percent of that is how you show up. The energy and leadership you embody.

In the rest of this book, I'm going to show you a way to let go of that Inner Friction, moment by moment, when it shows up.

Over time, using what I'm about to share with you will anchor in the awareness of your Divine Nature and your Frequency and identity as a transformational leader who makes seven figures. You'll sail through the "stuck points" and take action as the Version of You Who Already Has the Business.

These are the energetics of collapsing time.

Are you ready for it to be easier?

THE ENERGY OF "STANDARD"

What is the energy required to charge ultra-premium fees?

What is the energy of ultra-premium fees?

It was about ten days after the idea dropped in – the way that I was going to rebuild my business and uplevel my work. I was sitting at our dining room table, late, after everyone else had gone to bed, notebooks and old printed notes strewn around me, working out the program details so I could get down to the business of selling it.

The idea for the program was simple enough. For years, people had been asking me for a course on how to offer programs at $50k and up.

Going from charging by the hour for your coaching sessions to, say, $10k is one thing. I may have been one of the first to teach about that, but by this time, everyone and their mom was doing it.

But $50k was *edgy*.

Indeed, and not just "edgy" in theory. I don't know if you've ever mentored anyone to charge $50,000 for six months of service, but here's what happens:

People *freak out*.

And Brian has them running around in circles, thinking about anything other than their $50k program. So they won't really have to offer the $50k program.

"What will I offer everyone else?"

"I don't want to leave people behind!"

"OMG – I need a whole new business model."

"What's my down-sell?"

"I'm going to piss off everyone in my community."

"It's gross to charge that much. Oh, wait, I really should be charging that much!"

All of this, and so much more, had come up in every private client I'd ever mentored to offer $50ks or $100ks. The amount of paralysis was off the chain. By some miracle, they'd gotten results anyway.

But in that moment, I couldn't think of any of my coaching "power moves" that got them over the Inner Friction of charging $50k, so they could actually get it. And here I had the bright idea to mentor a lot more people to offer $50k programs in a way that was entirely new, and different from anything I'd ever seen before. This was my next step. And there was no getting around it.

Good golly, I thought. *I've got to come up with a way that people can instantly shift into be-ing the One Who Charges $50k and gets it. And it has to work so that they don't have to shift every damn block before they get started.*

So, I did what I always do, which is talk to the Goddess.

And she said, "Remember, Goddess, whatever they want already exists."

She said, "Whatever they need to *be*, just is."

It just is.

I smiled and began to channel.

THE THREE-WORD ENERGETIC "HACK" THAT MAKES EVERYTHING EASIER

One of my biggest struggles in life – which is also one of my greatest superpowers – is that I have a *very* activated emotional body. In other words – I am an empath times twenty. I feel all the feels, on overdrive, all the time.

When I became an entrepreneur, this was a *huge* struggle. And frankly, I was kind of ashamed. Because despite decades of the study of magic, and active priestess practice, I still didn't really have it handled.

A big part of this is because I'm a clear channel – an open channel. And I didn't want to shut that down. So, I worked with the tool that I had – and what all my early coaching mentors told me to work with – and that's *boundaries*.

To be clear – boundaries are 100 percent required. The problem, though, is how it made me *feel*.

Boundaries are great. They are satisfying. We need them. They also require energy. Hold the line. Yes or no. This is allowed or not allowed.

In business, there are a lot of boundaries to set. Boundaries with clients: this one wants out, this one wants special treatment, here's what we do in our program spaces, here's what we don't do. Boundaries with your team may look like: "No, you can't have that day off because we have a launch going on," "No, I'm not available for questions right now," "Yes, it's on you to figure it out."

Boundaries keep us healthy. They create the container. In cases of abuse and trauma, they heal deeply. Above all, boundaries keep things from descending into chaos. Obviously, this is a *good* thing,

All of that is fine and all, but when you're an energetic "open door" and you have a knack for attracting boundary pushers, including *yourself*, the constant setting of boundaries all the time gets exhausting.

As Tony Robbins says, the quality of your life is determined by the quality of the questions you ask. And so I asked a different question.

What if I didn't have to constantly "hold the boundaries"? What would that look like?

What if I could hold a boundary without all this block-and-tackle style, defensive energy?

Answer: "This just *is*."

Whatever is on the table, it's just how it is.

There's nothing to do. Nothing to fix. Nothing to change. Nothing to defend. Nothing to push against.

It just *is*.

For example, the law of gravity just *is* what it is. You can argue with it if you want, but gravity doesn't care. As one of my mentors, David Neagle, likes to say, "If you walk off the top of a building, you're going down."

Something that just is, is Truth.

Universal Truth just Is. And if it's Truth, then there's no negotiation. No division within yourself. No inner conflict. No friction.

It just *is*.

This is how it is, and that's how it is.

You know, like how your Divine Nature, your Highest Level, just *is*. It exists, whether you are aware of it or not.

That is the energy of holding a Standard.

The energy of "just is" is an energetic hack that will change your life. Because when you move from "push-pull," "will they, won't they," "can I, can't I," to the energy of "well, this just is," all resistance drops. You can align with and take action on Truth rather than illusion.

Notice that this is different than "standards" as we normally think of them. Hang out with coaches growing their business in the online space and you'll see what I mean. "Better boundaries," they say. "You've got to elevate what you're willing to tolerate. Change what you allow in your space. Hold the line. Raise your standards!"

Luckily, you don't have to "raise your standards" when you use the Standards. Because the Standards just are. Nothing to be, do fix, change, shift, uplevel, down level, cajole, push or force.

Whatever Standard you choose to hold, just *is*.

Glorious. Beautiful. Exhale.

THE TEN STANDARDS – THE FORMULA FOR YOUR SEVEN-FIGURE FREQUENCY

The Standards we'll cover in this book are a set of energies that we activate to embody the energy of a seven-figure transformational leader. If you're not "woo like me" (ha!), you might think of them as keys, or principles, or guidelines.

I like to think of them as energies. Because our Frequency isn't just made up of keys or principles. We don't manifest a seven-figure business with keys or principles, we manifest it through our Frequency. And our Frequency – that energy pattern that frees up your consciousness to perceive the opportunities to call in what you want (a seven-figure business in two years or less, in this case) – is a way of be-ing, not keys or principles that we get around to sometimes. And it's more than one thing.

Are there more than ten energies, or Standards, that could make up the vibrational signature, or way of be-ing the Version of You Who Has the Seven-Figure Business Already?

Absolutely. In fact, in addition to these ten, you'll have some Standards of your own – things that "just are" in your world.

What you'll find, though, is that these ten Standards – these ten energies, or ways of be-ing – are "the biggies" when it comes to being the One Who Has the Seven-Figure Business in the Now. They are definitely the biggies that have shown themselves in the fifteen-plus years that I've been teaching women entrepreneurs. And they're definitely the ones the Goddess Isis whispered to me at my dining room table that night.

They are:

- The Divine Standard
- The Abundance Standard
- The Confidence Standard
- The Expectation Standard
- The Discipline Standard
- The No Apologies Standard

- The Benevolent Queen Standard
- The Money Impeccability Standard
- The Transformation Standard
- The Frequency of Divine Love (The Secret Sauce)

We'll cover each of these in the chapters to come.

The thing about magic is, at the end of the day, it's pretty simple. Way simpler than Hollywood movies and the like would lead you to believe.

Magic is moving and directing energy. It's a shifting of energies from one form to another. Energy gets activated on both the physical (3D) and the non-physical (multidimensional) plane.

We activate energy on the non-physical plane with our intention. Universal Law tells us that energy always follows intent. What does this mean? Strikingly, it means that whatever you intend is *so*, on the non-physical planes. Intend it, and a mental picture gets formed. That mental picture is actually a *real thing*, in the non-physical dimensions.

On the physical realm – here where shit gets done, clients hire you, and seven-figure businesses get made – we activate specific energies (the Standards or otherwise) by action and embodiment.

We embody them by accepting and surrendering to the fact that each of them just *is*.

Already true. Already here.

It is done.

Throughout the book, I'll be showing you what this means for each of the Standards. Here's a simple example for now so you can contextualize and make the power of this real.

Let's say you were just contacted by a new potential client. A woman contacts you "out of the blue." But she isn't "out of the blue" to you; you've been stalking her for years. And now she wants to hire you? Or at least chat about it?

This *could* psych you out.

But instead, you activate the Confidence Standard. You remember that your mastery and the results you've already created, for yourself and others, already *are*. You remember that your awesomeness *just is*.

You chat over Messenger, hold a powerful space, and next thing ya know, she's in your $50k group.

You can show up *so* much more powerfully when you're connected to Truth. The Truth about You, and the Truth about your clients.

HERE'S WHAT THE STANDARDS ARE NOT...

I "downloaded" this system several years ago. Since that time, I have been nothing short of stunned at how the energetic shift "it just IS" (that is, shifting into embodying things that already are true) changes things for people and changes them *rapidly*.

And yet you should understand before going in what this work is about and what it is *not* about.

The work we're going to do is *not* more of "clear your blocks," though it will indeed clear blocks. It's *not* "reprogram your subconscious in a single session." Or "clear shit out at the root and it never comes up again."

You *will* reprogram yourself when you use the Standards. You'll do it through repetition and through creating *new* experiences that will anchor in the truths of the "just is-es."

There are two ways – and really, only two ways – that we change (i.e., make a transformation).

One is through peak experience. Those patterns that got fused in so long ago? Those happened in emotional moments, back when you were a child. The other is through repetition. Specifically, repetition that reaches your subconscious.

There are all kinds of very useful (and, dare I say, "cool") modalities out there that do either one or both of these. The Standards, however, work on the level of *conscious* awareness.

If you join one of our programs, including our course on the Standards, you'll see that we add some magic and subconscious reprogramming and other cool stuff.

But mostly, the Standards work their magic in the moment. They work by you bringing your awareness right back to the Truth of "It Just Is."

THE SECRET TRUTH OF TRANSFORMATION (SPOILER ALERT: IT'S NOT HARD)

Years ago, I had a conversation with a priestess. Ariel Spillsbury is a true elder, the founder of the Thirteen Moon Mystery School, an initiatory priestess path with active temples all over the world. Ariel is a woman you go to when you need clarity. Someone to help you see what you cannot.

Ariel is the Initiator. Not only will she see what you cannot... she'll call you out on everything you *are not* being, so you can snap back to the Truth.

At the time of our conversation, I was on the edge of a big leap. I was about to kick off a new program for our clients – a program that would become a multimillion-dollar revenue stream.

And damn, that Inner Friction had been getting in the way! I was terrified ... terrified of being "too big," terrified of being "too small," terrified of teaching the right things, terrified of accidentally teaching the "wrong" things. Old patterns were stopping me left and right.

We dropped into Presence together. The images started flowing. And the Goddess started talking.

"You are not allowing yourself to become a true empty channel for me," She said. "You are resisting what really wants to come through."

"Yeah, but I can't," I told her.

"You must."

A wave of sadness came over me. Sadness for all the times that I had said no. All the lost time. Missed opportunities. Fear.

Ariel would not let me tune out what the Goddess was saying. Where other facilitators would have hung back, she pounced.

"We are not f**king around here. This is very real. Are you willing to be that channel? Are you really going to say yes to that?

"This is a threshold that only you can cross. Only you can make that decision."

"But *how*?" I wailed.

"By saying yes to Her in every moment."

Naturally, I started bawling my head off. Then the Priestess spoke again, softer this time.

"I can tell you have been around the block with this 'not enough' stuff, the 'I'm too much for everyone,' too. What's it gonna take to let go of those *lies*?"

"Well, sh*t. I don't know," I said.

So, I asked Ariel a question that had been on my mind.

"Do you think we can change instantly? You know, do you think it's possible for us to just decide to let go of overeating or smoking or going into debt, or giving it all away to our clients, or making just enough to get by, or, or, whatever."

"Of course," she said. "See, that's the thing, Elizabeth. That's the thing about this question.

"It's not hard. It's simple. And it simply is *this*:

"There comes a point where you *choose* to have a shift in awareness.

"This is complete. I am Whole. It's a decision that it is done, it is done, it is done."

"Align with Truth. Shift it in the non-physical, and it replicates itself on the physical plane," I said. "As above, so below."

"That's right. You align with Truth. The shift happens on the upper planes and then on a cellular level. And that's it. It's over. It is done. The mind can't believe that it's so simple, but it really is. The rest is recalibrating – the physical body catching up to what has already happened.

"You can go around the block with shifting your blocks, Elizabeth. It's important work.

"At a certain point you just *decide* that it is *done*."

She had given me the secret to true soul-level change.

Our mind wants to make everything complicated. Our physical body will throw up interference of some kind. But none of that is real.

Soul-level change is instant. It starts with a decision. A clear decision within you, that you're going to make real on the outside.

Decide that you're "worth it."

Decide that you are enough.

Decide that you're doing it.

Decide that you're having it.

Decide that it is *done*.

The conscious awareness gets a bad rap in transformation. It's only 10 percent of your mind.

Well – it does a *lot*! It friggin' does a *lot*.

Conscious awareness is the catalyst for change.

And when you recognize a situation in which a Standard is required, in the moment, you'll see it, and you'll go, "Oh, yeah, this just *is*," and you'll relax.

You may have more blocks to shift, more wounds to heal, things to "fix" about yourself, and things to fix about your business. None of that changes the fact that you are coded for success, and your soul-level Desires are already done in the non-physical, and all that's left to do is bring them into the 3D realm.

By using the Standards, you can relax into that Truth, and stop fighting your success so much.

Are you ready for it to be easier?

Let's begin.

4

THE DIVINE STANDARD

For as long as I can remember, I have been fascinated with personal transformation – how we change, why we change, why we don't change. And why change can feel so hard.

As a budding magician (as a witchlet running around New York City, learning magic in my early twenties), I knew, intellectually, that change is possible. I saw some awe-mazing magicians do some crazy amazing things.

At the same time, I saw others stay stuck. Do "all the magic" and yet still struggle with the basics of life.

So, when I asked Ariel the question, it was a real revelation.

"There comes a point where you *choose* to have a shift in awareness. A point where you say:

'I am Whole.

'This is complete.

'It is done, it is done, it is done.'"

"Well, why is it so hard to do that, then?" I asked.

She told me that, well, actually, it's *not* "so hard" to do that. It's not hard at all, when you're willing to let go of the idea that it has to be hard.

"Elizabeth, it's a decision."

The very second we make a decision, it is, in a very real way, done. Because if we've truly made a decision, it by definition means that we have *released* all the other options.

If that is so, then we have truly already *manifested* it, which is a very powerful place to be.

THE TWO HALVES OF "THE MANIFESTING EQUATION"

Of course, there are always umpteen possible reasons why manifesting isn't working as you expect it to. But, all of them basically boil down to the same reason.

When we manifest, we need to understand what I call "the two halves of the manifesting equation."

On the one hand, we have the Divine Side – the "spiritual superpowers" side. The Law. Your Highest Level Self. Your Divine Nature. The fact that you're God / Goddess, and, therefore, you have *pow-ah*. The quantum realms and multidimensionality and all that cool stuff.

Most manifesting courses focus almost exclusively on the Divine side. Work with the energy! Embody your vibration! Law of Attraction! All that.

At the same time, most neglect to adequately lay out or address the other side of the manifesting equation. The other side that impacts it.

The Human side. Your Human Nature. The fact that sure, you may be "God" and all ... but you're also having a *human experience.*

Being human means that you have a brain that is very, very invested in *you* staying exactly as you are. Maintaining the status quo or "safe state" is the brain's number one priority.

The triune brain theory is an evolutionary theory that says our brain has three parts, each developed at different times. The first is the brainstem – what I like to think of as the "lizard brain." This is the part of the brain that is tracking our vital signs, making sure our heart is still beating, and similar. It's also the part of the brain that makes us run, or fight, or freeze when a woolly mammoth happens by.

Then, there's the limbic brain – the emotional brain. This is the part of the brain that likes to feel warm and fuzzy. It's not unlike a puppy who wants to curl up with you after it hasn't seen you for a long day.

Finally, there's the neocortex – the logical brain. This brain thrives on order! This is the Brain of the Ego. It figures shit out, *and* it is the brain that is connected to the Higher Realms, the place where intuition resides.

There's a really interesting thing that goes on with the brains – interesting, but also a bummer, because it sets up the conflict for humans that makes us miserable our entire lives.

Your neocortex – that big ol' smart brain – is always reaching for the stars, so to speak. This is the aspirational brain, the brain that can form visions, and the brain that is inspired to follow them. The part of our brain that Desires and *goes* for it.

Unfortunately, it's living right alongside the brain stem. The brain stem has other ideas. The brain stem's *sole point in life* is to keep us from death. Its biggest goal is: Don't die.

Indeed, this is such a big deal for the brain stem that its whole job in life is to walk around checking in to see if we're dead yet and, if we're not dead, to keep on doing the things that made us *not dead* – even if they kind of suck for us.

Snacking when you're bored? That kept us from death last time, so let's do it again. Buying designer handbags to make us feel whole? Great idea! And, oh, yeah, we were able to survive that narcissistic mother just fine, so let's find a life partner who is just like our mom – that way we can keep on living.

This makes *zero* sense to our higher mind, of course – but it makes *loads* of sense to the critter brain!

And you can see how it sets us up for trouble.

This conflict between our Higher Mind, our neocortex, and our Lower Mind or lizard brain, the brain stem, keeps us in constant tug of war. One part of us is *pushing* us (from the inside) to *go for it*! While another part of us is telling us to put the brakes on. Plus, that part of us telling us to put the brakes on has adopted all kinds of patterns designed to keep us exactly where we are.

(When we at 7-Figure Goddess® speak about Brian, and what Brian has us doing, we are essentially referring to all the fun things that arise from this conflict.)

This, my dear Goddess, is our *human* side. And in order to fully activate our co-creative powers, we must learn how to dance with *both*.

A NEW AWARENESS

In the personal development world, we focus a lot on healing our "inner human." Breaking patterns, busting through blocks, shifting our mindset, healing our trauma, and so on.

But we can get *stuck* on the deep healing, spending way too much time here, all the while forgetting the magic of simple awareness – awareness of our Divine

Nature, especially – and really not getting that we have one.

We can get so fascinated by hanging out on the healing journey that we *forget* the awareness part, or we never knew the awareness part and how *simple* that is.

And this is what we do with the Standards. The Standards are a new awareness. Having the awareness of a Truth and stepping fully into it *now*.

Not later. Now.

Years ago, one of my mentors described awareness as "the catalyst for change." I've always loved that, and found myself using the phrase, because it's true.

And, we can go farther. Magicians know that awareness isn't *just* the catalyst for change.

What Ariel was trying to tell me (cut through the fog and tell me) is that awareness isn't just a catalyst for change. It *is* the change.

I had to laugh, because magicians have known this for years. "Change in accordance with Will" is a common definition of magic.

The faster we shift into the awareness, embody it fully, and stay there, the faster the change we are looking for … just happens.

"WHAT'S IT GOING TO TAKE?"

After Ariel gave it to me straight, I asked, "Well, what now? Like, after we make the decision and poof the change is done, what then? How do we get the body to catch up?"

And she says, "You know what? Put sticky notes on the mirror."

And I'm thinking, *put sticky notes on the mirror?* You have two big books of transmissions you downloaded and a tradition that you founded in Hawaii that has become this global thing, and you're telling me to put sticky notes on the mirror? *This* is your big transformational move?

And she's like, "Yeah. Remind the brain. It is *done.*"

And then she added, "Sister, what's it gonna take?"

As magicians – and if you're an experienced coach, healer, teacher, conscious expert, you *are* a magician – this is hugely important for us to really *get*.

We want to honor the body. We want to honor our critter brain. We want to honor all three brains. Sometimes there is more busting blocks and mindset shifting and transformation to *do*.

And nonetheless, the big secret of magic is that it's already *done*.

The work of magic, in my experience – and really the work of working with the Standards, is *living into* what is already *done*.

And *why* it matters is because we manifest by way of opportunities dished up through the Field. Our

Alignment with "it just is" and "It's already done" *completely determines* what we see.

A Course in Miracles (which, by the way, I am only slightly familiar with) says, "A miracle is a shift in perception."

Guess what? Same thing.

In his book *Think and Grow Rich*, Napoleon Hill says, "Most people never lift themselves high enough to *see* success." Ouch, right?

Well, what he's really saying is most peeps don't raise their consciousness – their awareness – to a level where they can see the opportunities that are all around them.

When you truly understand that your Divine Nature already exists, and that that which you seek is already there – your seven-figure business – and take action from *that* place rather than from the fears that Brian feeds you, you align with the Frequency of Truth rather than illusion.

And the biggest Truth of all, the big reveal of the ages, is *Thou Art Goddess*.

You are Divine. You are not separate from Source. You originated from the Field. You are from it, and of it, and share its nature.

This is a very, very old metaphysical secret, one that I believe deserves to be "out there," out of the initiates' chambers. Because we – the greater collective – need *all* of you, now.

Deep breath. Be patient with yourself if you have to just *be* with this one for a hot minute.

With the Standards, our goal – if you choose to accept it – is to move the awareness of "Thou Art Goddess" from an intellectual one to something that lives within you. To hold that *truth* as the Truth.

And it *is* a choice.

(In any of my spaces, including this book, you are always at choice. At any point, if what I say simply does not resonate, you are more than welcome to put the book down, and I will still be grateful to have had the ability to serve you in any way that I have.)

The Divine Standard is holding the awareness of one's Divine Nature as Truth, no matter what. And to use that awareness to create anything you want, really.

Here in this book, our goal is for you to use that awareness to give yourself a different experience in your business – to move from struggling and pushing and driving and striving to ease and flow and grace and miracles. You know, most of the time.

Throughout the rest of this chapter, we're going to break down the implications of the Divine Standard – what it really means for you. Because when you really take on your Divinity as the Standard – the way things are, something that just is and that's the way it is (because, you know, it is) – there are huge, positive, rock-your-world implications.

Like all of the Standards, the Divine Standard is a

shift in awareness. It can, and does, happen in an instant.

It is a choice.

You don't have to go do a bunch more healing, you don't have to turn yourself into a project, you don't have to make yourself bad or wrong for being human.

You just remember what you already know to be true, what already is.

WHAT FOLLOWS FROM THE DIVINE STANDARD #1

When I understand that Thou Art Goddess, I no longer accept the lies that the Monkey Mind feeds me about me.

I don't need to tell you that our minds are a *hotbed* of illusion lies.

They keep us stuck because we accept them as truth.

They're *not* truth.

It's very likely that you already know this. This is personal development 101.

If you're hearing this Truth for the first time, I am so glad to be the one to bring it to ya!

Here's the news: your thoughts, feelings, and perceptions are not Truth.

Our thoughts and feelings are generated by stories

that we were either told long ago or that we made up long ago in order to survive. They are our filter through which we see the world.

My question to you is: Why are you putting up with the lies? Why are you still accepting stories as your truth?

It's time for a new Standard. Tell yourself the Truth.

Sure, the lies may still be there. It's very likely they're still going to be there – brains being brains after all.

But when you hold the Divine Standard, you're not energizing them. When you hold the Divine Standard, you say, "I am not accepting them as my Truth."

The Truth is – I am Goddess. I am Divine. I easily create big goals in alignment with my soul and in a way that brings more life to all.

Most of the Standards are about telling yourself the Truth.

Hold the Standard and we can instantly let the lies go.

WHAT FOLLOWS FROM THE DIVINE STANDARD #2

When I understand that Thou Art Goddess and so is everybody else, I no longer accept the lies that the Monkey Mind feeds me about others.

Your clients. Your Team. Your parents. Your fifth-grade teacher who was a total shithead. Your cat Mittens, who was your cat in the fifth grade and was a total asshole.

None of the bullshit is true.

They might be presenting as total pains in your ass. You may have a lot to say about it, lots of stories to tell. But it's not how they *are*. And it's your *brain* – our old friend Brian – telling those stories, not you.

This is important. Because when we switch into – "I can see the Divine in you" (clients, team, parents, cat, etc.), then we are no longer in a place of "I am *fighting* you."

We can get so angry and project and get pissed – and that hurts *us*.

Now, of course, hurt people hurt people. Nobody gets to a place where they are building a seven-figure business, say, without having some major shit in their lives – and shit done *to* them. There are stories, and there are *facts*.

Seeing the Divinity in others is not about giving those who hurt us a "free pass" or ignoring wrongs that must be acknowledged and, if possible, righted. That's called bypass, and it serves no one.

We can be in a place of compassion without bypassing. We can set the required boundaries (yes, boundaries) with those who hurt us. We can preserve our peace.

When you really *get* that Thou Art Goddess – and your *clients* are, too – what does that do?

You instantly see them as the powerful be-ings they are. What happens when you see them as powerful? They rise. (We are going to talk about this a lot more in the chapter on the Expectation Standard.)

It also makes difficult conversations much, much easier.

WHAT FOLLOWS FROM THE DIVINE STANDARD #3

When I understand that Thou Art Goddess and so is everybody else, I understand that I am not my patterns, mistakes or past, and neither is anybody else.

If you're a parent, you've seen how easy it is for kids to equate their behavior with themselves. Frankly, it's heartbreaking. And it's just as messed up when we carry the same habit (product of an underdeveloped brain) into adulthood, way after our brains are fully developed.

You are not your mistakes. You are not your patterns. Neither are other people.

In Feminine Magic® (our metaphysical teach-ings), we have a practice of honoring what is. We honor what is because we want to stay in rapport with what is. Because when we are not in rapport with what is, we are rejecting essential parts of ourselves. And that becomes a costly form of self-annihilation.

For example, about a year and a half after we had our daughter Brigit, I discovered that I have a deep wound around relationships. I also discovered how it had totally messed up my life up until that point. It almost ruined my marriage.

My husband and I went on the deep dive. Therapy, plus – you guessed it – a fair amount of neuro-linguistic programming (NLP) on my side.

The whole healing process took about six months, with maybe another year to integrate and recalibrate.

One of my dear friends, a powerful mindset coach whose strategy involves being fierce about her words and stories, admonished me once.

"You keep talking about this like a badge of honor. Stop talking about it! You're just holding on to it!"

That's fair on one hand. A lot of storytelling will drive said story further into your neurology.

But the facts on the ground are: this is my experience and it has shaped who I am. Why would I want to reject that part of myself? How on earth could that be a good idea?

But it's not me. The Divine Standard tells me that, in a heartbeat.

When we hold the Divine Standard, we activate

an *instant* unhooking from illusions. The parts of you that you "don't like," the wounds, the dysfunctional patterns, the adaptive strategies, the coping mechanisms, may be a part of your experience and a part of who you are, but they are not Who You Are.

The limitations you think are there on your growth aren't really there!

They may be a part of your experience, but we don't have to make them *all the thing.*

When we unhook from illusion, and see our patterns for what they are, we have a direct line to more Truth.

WHAT FOLLOWS FROM THE DIVINE STANDARD #4

When I understand that Thou Art Goddess and so is everybody else, I no longer have to prove my worth, in or out of business.

If Thou art Goddess, you instantly have value. Your value isn't even a question. Your value is a fact. So instead of having to prove your worth and your value, you can just get into a groove with seeing how much value you can *create* and *provide* in the world.

Spoiler Alert: You make money in your business by providing *value, not* by doing a bunch of gyrations to prove your worth or value.

There's nothing to prove. Your value just *is*.

When you truly hold the Divine Standard, you start to break out of overdelivering, over-justifying, overselling (this is a big one), overexplaining, and bending over backward to get peeps into your programs.

Instead, you begin to see your programs as brilliant offerings that are perfect for the right person. You don't have to "sell" them. But you DO have to hold the leadership frequency *and* clearly communicate what they are getting.

Imagine a banquet table and it is spread with *the* ideal feast that your clients want.

Let's say you're vegan, your clients are vegan, and that table is piled high with raw vegan superfoods and colorful salads, and someone made vegan cake, and there's green juice with just the right amount of sweetness, and in the center there's a big sign that says, "Vegan smorgasbord."

You're *not* going to have to sell that to a hungry vegan. A hungry vegan is going to come up to you and say, "I'm starving," and when you make them an offer they can't refuse, they say, "Here's my money."

Everything we do in 7-Figure Goddess® on the strategy side of things is like that. Your energy is standing in your power, in front of your laid- out table, going, "Here's my table, would you like to come sit at my table?"

WHAT FOLLOWS FROM THE DIVINE STANDARD #5

When I understand that Thou Art Goddess and so is everybody else, I can much more easily accept large amounts of money from other people.

When you accept that Thou Art Goddess and everyone else is too, it makes it *much* easier to accept large amounts of money from other people.

When we start out in business, most of us hate selling. We have an adverse reaction to selling.

Once again, this has nothing to do with us. Did you know that in every major religion's major text, there is at least *one* story of someone meeting their doom because of a sale? Think: Adam and Eve.

With disdain for selling so deeply coded in us, it's no wonder that most of us have to get over massive "stuff" around it. For many of us, selling feels like we're taking. Harming. And then, at a certain point, when we realize that there's no eating without selling and that all money moves as a result of sales, we get over this once we get comfortable with charging. But you can still be charging a lot and undercharging.

When I understand that Thou Art Goddess and so is everybody else, I understand that I could never harm or take, provided that I am acting for More Life and the good of all. I can never harm or take when I allow others free will.

When I understand that Thou Art Goddess and so is everybody else, I understand that that money is not money coming *from* my clients. It's coming from Source *through* them.

Obviously, we want to remember and have deep respect for what that money represents, and what it actually is. Money is the energy of someone's life minutes, their consciousness, their hopes, dreams, and so on. We honor that, while receiving our part in the exchange. You're a Divine Being, and they are a Divine Being, and you're playing a role in each other's evolution.

WHAT FOLLOWS FROM THE DIVINE STANDARD #6

When I understand that Thou Art Goddess and so is everybody else, I understand that I have instant availability and access to more resources than I ever could have imagined before.

The Truth is – I am Goddess. I am Divine. I easily create *big* goals in alignment with my soul and in a way that brings more life to *all*.

You're already a powerful creator. How could you *not* be?

In a forthcoming chapter, we will cover the Abundance Standard. Spoiler alert: the Abundance Standard tells us that infinite abundance just *is*. (The Law backs this up, as you'll see.)

"Know your Supply." Your supply is Source, and it comes *through* other people. Source being Source and all, the supply is therefore infinite.

An understanding and acceptance of your Divine Nature instantly gives you access to *more* – more resources, more opportunities, more paths to manifest.

WHAT FOLLOWS FROM THE DIVINE STANDARD #7

When I understand that Thou Art Goddess and so is everybody else, I know without a shadow of a doubt that it's already here and already done.

And here might be the very best, most fun aspect of the Divine Standard. Let's get down to brass tacks. Let's instantly put all the possibilities and chips on the table.

Your big income goal is already a done deal.

Of course, you'll figure out the strategy because *of course*.

Of course, you'll call in a team of highly aligned rock stars because of course.

It doesn't matter if the last email "worked" or not because it's done.

And you *don't* have to figure it all out!

When Thou Art Goddess and "it just is" – you stay out of having to get all caught up in the minutiae of all the things in your business. You still get to figure out the strategy, you still have to train the team, you still have to deal with all the things that come up.

But you have a way to *instantly* shift out of those things pulling on you – the need to *know* pulling on you.

One of the things I've come to learn over the years is that whenever my brain is straining to "figure it out," it is simply resisting the fact that it does not know a given thing – yet.

Who cares about knowing the how!

Focus on the outcome, for it is already done.

In my experience, the biggest impediment to manifesting is the *perception of lack*. Most people go through their lives trying to "get." Most business owners do, too. They have to "get" the clients. "Get" the money. Get, get, get.

When the brain goes into having to "get," it's because there is some part of us that thinks we *don't have*. In that moment, we are in a lack vibration. And it's almost impossible to manifest from that place.

The good news is, it's always already here, so, you

know, you can just shift out of that instantly with a single awareness.

Peeps who are comfortable charging a ton of money understand that the money is flowing to and through them – from Source. Flows from Source through people and then to other people through *them*.

WHAT FOLLOWS FROM THE DIVINE STANDARD #8

When I understand that Thou Art Goddess and so is everybody else, I can be in deep connection with myself, with others, and the world.

Peter J. Reding, the founder of Coach for Life, has a quote I just love: "There is only one problem, and that is separation. There is only one solution, and that is connection."

When we see that we come from the same Source, we can face the very real challenges of our world – including injustice and systems of oppression that continue to stand – head on, straight in the eyes and hold spiritual Truth at the same time.

We can create change on the micro level, one person and interaction at a time.

The Divine Standard invites you to continue to

heal inner wounds of separation. It brings you into deep connection with the world because aligning with this Standard invites you to see that all of your clients, team, mentors, teachers, parents, people who trigger you, and even those who have hurt you have a Divine Aspect, too.

The Divine Standard evens the playing field, while acknowledging that there is still work to be done, rights to wrong, wounds to heal, and injustices to be made right. Ultimately, it invites you to see that you are enough and that everyone in your world is enough, too.

When we come from a place of connection and enough-ness, we can collapse time.

One of my favorite mentors tells the story of her first million-dollar year. She struggled with "enough" all year long. Every week, she would look at the results in her business and beat herself up. This was wrong, that was wrong … it was never enough.

She chose a million-dollar year, but by the end of July, only brought in $149,000.

Something inside of her cracked open. She took out a sticky note and wrote, "I am enough."

By the end of November, she had generated over $800,000, and had a million-dollar year.

When we align with the Truth that we are Divine and so is everybody else, and truly hold that for ourselves, we can allow the lies to fall away and for

Spirit to work to and through us, to bring our visions to life.

We can wait, or we can call it in quickly, because it's here now.

Which will you choose?

5

THE ABUNDANCE STANDARD

S o let's talk about cash infusions. Or anything else you want to create.

I'll use high-end programs as our context because that's what I've been mentoring on since 2008.

The Standards came to be because I was being asked to teach on how to offer $50k programs with integrity. Teach on high-end at any fee, and there's a question that everyone is dying to ask.

Where are they?

In all my years of teaching high-end, this was always either the number one or number two *"yeahbut."* "Yeahbut, where are the clients" or "Yeahbut, my clients won't pay for that" – which is really another way of saying, "Yeahbut where are the clients."

And really, it's the same for any manifesting goal

you have. Teach manifesting, and you'll discover that the first thing peeps want to know is the *how*. "How, how, how, how, how?"

"Where are they?" is just another variation of this. With high-end clients, specifically, let's go ahead and answer that.

Your $50k clients are wherever you're currently going to magnetize clients.

If your marketing jam is Facebook, they're on Facebook. If you're on LinkedIn, they're on LinkedIn. If you're on Instagram, they're on Instagram. If you're going to events, they're at events. They are *definitely* at events.

So – unless you're talking about switching to an entirely different clientele (like, say, you're shutting down your financial planning business to open a dog walking business), your clients are where you're already looking. Plus, wherever else they may be that you're not looking yet.

Our business is *full* of examples of this. Here's one.

One of my private clients had decided to make a new $50k offer that reflects what she really wanted to do – what we call her Highest Level Transformation. She has been zipping along offering $10ks and $50ks for a while, but she wasn't really excited about the work.

It was one of those things where she was being called into the next level of her work. As such, there was a whole new type of client she wanted to work with: celebrities and creatives.

"I'm so over the coaches who coach coaches coaching coaches," she said.

"So go get your new person," I answered.

"I don't think my people are on Facebook." (Note: Facebook is where she hangs out most of the time.) "If I want to meet my ideal people, I'm going to have to go by referral."

"Maybe, *and* some of your clients are here on Facebook in the same old places where you've been marketing for the past two years."

She set a seemingly impossible goal of $150k in two weeks. She booked $120k. All were her new ideal client. All came from her posts on Facebook. Which brings us to The Abundance Standard.

YOUR SUPPLY IS TRULY UNLIMITED

The Abundance Standard is holding yourself in alignment with the *Divine Truth* that there is no lack, only abundance.

Truth is Abundance.

Or, as we like to say in Feminine Magic®: *Your Supply is truly unlimited.*

Let's take a minute and break this down. Because – surprise, surprise – there are a couple of Universal Laws at play. One of them is the Law of Supply.

When we wish to manifest anything – more

clients, more money, more opportunities, a seven-figure business with ease and grace, first we must know our Supply.

What is Supply?

To put it simply, our Supply is The Thinking Stuff from Which All Things Are Made, Creative Substance, Creative Life Force Energy, Divine Energy.

If everything is energy, and we are surrounded by, and are an extension of, the Creative Substance, then there is no end to the Creative Substance. It is formless, limitless, without ceasing.

Therefore, your Supply is truly unlimited.

Therefore, metaphysically speaking and yet in a very real way, there is no lack.

Now, we need to be careful here, so we are not ignoring the realities of the world we live in. The world we live in is *full* of lack circumstances. Millions upon millions of people live in lack circumstances and experience lack every day.

These are the facts. The physical plane reality. I would never deny that fact, and neither should you.

Spiritually speaking, however, there is no lack. This Truth is the key behind the Abundance Standard.

The Law of Supply tells us that everything comes from Source. Source is infinite, which means your Supply is infinite.

That's the first aspect of the Laws that underlie the Abundance Standard. That Truth would be powerful enough – life-changing. But there's another Law that is even more impactful and life-changing – indeed, there is another Law that tells us that not only is there *truly no lack*, only lack-based circumstances, but also that manifesting any and ALL of your Desires is a done deal, if you allow them to be.

And that is...

Everything you truly Desire is already here.

When I speak of Desire (capital D Desire, rather than "desire") – I am speaking of something very specific. I am speaking of the true Desires of your heart. Those things that your soul is truly longing for. What your neocortex, which has a direct line to the heavens, is seeking. The Desires that are pointing you in the direction of your life purpose.

In other words, if, say, you're seventy years old and all of a sudden want to "bet the Universe" that you could be a professional ballet dancer and you're a rank beginner, well, that's not a soul-level desire. That's betting the Universe.

When you are not betting the Universe, and your creative impulse, the Desires of your heart are leading you to create a seven-figure business in record time, there is something very important that you need to know and understand and why.

Everything you want is already here.

It's already here. Already manifested. Already done.

If you're new to my teachings, you will hear me talk about this over and over and over and *over* again. Indeed, we've already touched on it.

This is the Law of Polarity. And the Law of Polarity tells us that there are no "halves" in the Universe.

Consider this...

There is no "up" without a "down." You can't have an "in" without an "out," a "front" without a "back," or a "black" without a "white."

If I was to hold a sheet of paper out in front of you, there'd be no arguing that there are two sides to that paper.

Everything has two sides. There are no halves, there are no single sides. And that means...

You cannot have a Desire for a thing without the way for it to be made manifest to also be present. What's more, the *way* is in your field.

That is to say, if you want to make $150k in a couple of weeks, and you want it to come through private programs in your business (let's say), those clients are already here. They are in your world. They're within spitting distance.

It can't *not* be... for this is Law.

Now, there's another implication, or shade, of the Law of Polarity that is also important to know, and that is:

A Desire is not felt by a human being until the way for it to be made manifested is present.

The supply is not present until the demand for that supply is also present; if the demand is present, so must be the supply.

That which you seek is also seeking you. You have the Desire; the demand is there.

This means... you want the $100k cash infusion? It's a true Desire of your heart?

(And you can just want it, by the way – there doesn't have to be some noble reason for it to be the Desire of your heart.)

It's already here.

The $17k clients? They're already here.

The seven-figure business delivering your Great Work to your perfect- fit, Next Level clients?

Already here. Totally possible. Already done.

And you don't have to "work" or "hustle" to have it, either! Because that's the thing we always hear, "Oops, I don't want to hustle! I'm not going to do it!"

Great! Don't do it! Don't hustle! You don't have to hustle all the time. That's a thing your human brain created from a belief that isn't accurate.

So that's the second bit – the second reason why Truth is Abundance.

This is the biggie. The Law of Polarity basically gives us the keys to the kingdom. The Law of Polarity says that there is pretty much nothing that you cannot manifest, and that whatever you want, you can have it – provided that you're willing to get the hell over yourself and get out of your own way. (There's the rub, as the saying goes.)

Finally, we've got one more Law for ya – that is, one more bit of really good news…

The First Law of the Universe is *more*. More Life.

More life to all, less to none.

More life equals *supply*. This is why we have enterprising entrepreneurs working away at something BEFORE there is a demand for it in the public consciousness.

Honestly, I could not imagine a world without a service like Uber. I take Ubers all the time. Well before I thought it was even possible, the Uber dude was noticing what a pain in the bum-bum it was to get a taxi, tuning in to the collective consciousness, and coming up with a solution to a problem that none of us even were aware that we had yet.

Supply meets the Demand. If there is Demand, there is also Desire – a.k.a. Supply.

Supply is infinite because Creative Substance is also infinite. There is no end to the Field.

And another thing. We are programmed for *more*.

I didn't make this up. You know how Joseph Campbell talks about finding your Bliss? Your Bliss is lots of things; one of those things is the urge for More, the Desire for More, the Desire for growth.

The evolutionary psychologists and biologists I

know call this urge "the Evolutionary Impulse." The Desire to grow, expand, develop, move forward.

Every living creature has this. We all have the impulse within us that seeks to be, do, and have More.

Our Desires are the urge for More Life, seeking fuller expression. You want more because you are programmed for more.

Because we are programmed for *more*, there can be no truth of "lack" or we'd very quickly extinguish ourselves.

LACK-BASED CIRCUMSTANCES ARE REAL (AND THERE IS NO PARADOX IN THIS)

Now, I know what you're thinking. Or might be thinking. This line of thinking frazzles the mind when it first hears it.

So I want to be clear: when we discuss the Laws, we *never* overlook lack circumstances.

The zero bank account balance you may have had at your lowest point was very real. As I speak, there are millions of people in poverty or war, and they are dying.

That's a fact.

You've all felt lack circumstances – you're feeling it every day! We're all walking around with it, even those of us with millions of dollars.

"I can't find the team." "Where are the clients?!"

And this is the problem.

Our minds *confuse* lack-based circumstances with spiritual lack.

But the Divine Truth says there is no lack. Divine Truth is abundance.

But spiritually speaking, there is no lack.

This means that if you have a sincere Desire for a certain amount of money, the *way* for it to be made manifest is here already. The money is already here.

It also means that the two sides of a thing exist *simultaneously*.

Where the experience of lack is present, abundance is also present.

If you Desire $100k right now, the WAY for it to be made manifest is *also* here.

By Law, it has to be there.

The problem is you don't see it, yet.

But it's here, and you can count on that as sure as the sun rises.

What does that allow you to do? Get out of lack-based thinking and lack-based energy. You can stop freaking out about money not being here.

When you *truly* get that everything is already here, you don't have to go around worrying about money and where's my money and all that. It's already here. It *has* to be.

Using this truth – *all* of the Standards – allows us to shift our *physical* experience powerfully and rapidly.

With the Abundance Standard, we take the Truth of Abundance and *embody it.*

We commit to shifting *out* of the illusion of lack. The truth of abundance becomes our new standard. Abundance just is.

The difference with the Abundance Standard, though, is that we are *fierce* about it.

When Abundance is the standard, we fiercely eliminate any thoughts to the contrary.

This means: You have value. Your ideas have value. People want your stuff

Someone wants your Highest Level work already. The clients are here, the money is here.

It just is, and it is here, now.

It is done.

Now fiercely shifting out of the illusion of lack does *not* mean you just sit around on the couch and expect the gold ingots to rain down on your head.

It also *doesn't* mean that you sit back and just let clients "come to you."

The Field operates completely deductively. As we discussed in Chapter 1, it can only give back to you in alignment with the vibrational signature you put into it.

This means you must impress the Field with the vibrational signature that is aligned with what you are calling in.

Does that mean a lot of "doing"? No.

Sometimes, there is "doing." If we want to create

in the physical, there are always aligned actions to take (including a big one, which I will share below).

Brian – our brains - gets confused. Brian hears this and goes into panic mode. "I don't want to hustle! I'm not going to burn myself out again!"

If you can relate, I am going to lovingly offer the possibility that as a master magician and grown-ass adult, it's time to let go of the knee-jerk reaction to the possibility of "hustle."

Why? Because as a grown-ass adult, you don't want to be ruled by some guy named Brian. (You don't want to be ruled by your reactions.)

As a master magician, you know that the way of easeful manifestation is to have the Truth on the table, and as many possibilities as possible.

So, aligned action impresses the Field. And the Field has *no choice* but to do what?

Bring you the opportunities. In alignment with your vibration and your current level of awareness.

"I don't want to *hustle!*" is an example of another important understanding you'll need, if you want to create a cash infusion or anything else you want.

Here it is: your thoughts, feelings, and perceptions are not Truth.

Brian will feed us information that there is *lack*. Brian wants us to think of that as Truth.

It's not Truth. It's a circumstance. Those things are different.

Here's the thing about the Law of Polarity: you will also see evidence of the *other* side.

When you go for something, you will see the evidence of *not* having it. The *opposite* of your intention will show up. And the reason why is because your subconscious mind goes around looking for evidence to prove itself right.

Your Desire – your neocortex – says, "Hey, I want this, and I know it's already here!"

Meanwhile your brain stem – your critter brain – is literally wired to go around looking for evidence that reinforces the belief systems it has that are there to keep you in a safe state – that is, the same.

Brian wants you to believe that want you see is all there is.

It's *not* all there is. You cannot see everything that there is because you're operating in a current level of awareness. But that doesn't mean that it's *not there*.

Truth is Abundance.

Truth is that it's *got* to be here. It *has* to be.

Believe me, I get how infuriating this is. Back in the days when I had nothing in the bank account, and no skills in this area, my mentor David would say, "Your empty bank balance is just a perception." And I would think, *are you friggin' kidding me right now?!*

That *is* a circumstance. The bank balance is at *zero*. But that's *not all there is*.

Know your *supply*. Your supply is unlimited.

I know the Truth and the Truth is abundance. Period. End of. And I will take aligned action accordingly.

Another one of my mentors, Travis Sago, is truly one of the most abundant people I have ever met, one of the happiest and one of the most abundant. When I met him early on, one of the things he said was, "Elizabeth, money is like oxygen. When I take a breath – inhale – I'm not worried about my oxygen supply, am I? Why would I do that? Why on earth would money be any different?"

It's already here. It matches your level of awareness. And your awareness can shift in an instant.

Remember, both states (lack and abundance, in this case) are present at the same time.

That being the case, notice that we have a choice.

If the *opposite* of what you Desire shows up, one of the reasons why it's doing so is because your mind is programmed to see "the old way."

We can see these "failures" as failure or a sign that "it's not here yet." Or we can see it as a sign that the Law is operating flawlessly.

When we see "failures," that means that the opposite of failure, your Desire, is also here.

It's here! Giving you the opportunity to detach from the pain of "not having it" yet.

When everything you want is already here, you can be in the energy of surety that you have it. We can let go of this notion that we don't have it. We can look to the obstacle as the way *through* to have what we want.

WHAT YOU GET TO LET GO OF WHEN YOU HOLD "ABUNDANCE" AS YOUR STANDARD

The first thing you get to let go of when holding the Abundance Standard is any form of money drama. We'll get into that in the chapter on the Money Impeccability Standard.

Second thing: you get to let go of comparison. This is huge.

If we look at comparison, what is that?

Beliefs: "I can't have it / do it / be it because she's already doing it."

"She's doing it so much better than me, I'll never measure up."

None of that is true. And like shame, comparison is a great way for your mind to give you a bypass.

Third thing we get to give up with the Abundance Standard: either- or thinking. "I can have my clients, [which is really 'I can have love'], *or* the $50k"; "I can have high-end, *or* low end."

Well, those are crappy choices. How about *both*?

"I can have a million dollars, or I can run myself into the ground." Well, that *sucks*. How about a seven-figure biz that is light and joyful and fun and simple to run?

Yes, and. And you can think of others.

The *real* key to "light and joyful and fun and simple to run" is to enjoy every freaking minute of the journey instead of what you *think* it's gonna take from you. Or what you *think* it's gonna cost you.

What is that? Lack.

Another thing: "Have to." "Well, if I want to create X, I 'have to' all this stuff."

There is only *one* "have to," really – and that is growth. If you wish to create, you will be asked (by Source, by those you serve, by *yourself*) to *grow*.

Fiercely embodying the Abundance Standard equals *freedom*. It's a practice because we are *so* conditioned for lack in the collective. But conditioning can be transformed into something else. If you can condition your mind to see lack, you can condition your mind for abundance.

Whatever you're calling in is here now. It will come in as quickly as you're willing to receive it.

WHAT ACTIVATES SUPPLY COMING TOWARD YOU: A DECISION

There is a lot to the Abundance Standard – much more than we can cover in this short introduction! And so many different ways to work with it, too.

One thing that they all have in common, is the one thing, above all else, that activates the Abundance Standard. The one thing that activates all that you Desire coming to you: a clear decision that it is *done*, and that you are having it.

Entrepreneurs sometimes groan when we talk about the importance of decisions. The root of the word "decide" means "to cut off all other options."

Do we really need to cut off all the options? I mean, isn't manifestation about allowing in more options?

Well, yes. And yes!

The fact is, The Field does *not* have any reason to bring anything to you without a decision. Remember: it can *only* give back to you what you impress on *it*. It literally can't do anything else.

As for options, we already have infinite options before we decide. Your possibilities are really only limited to what you can imagine, as a Desire of your heart.

Sure, not every manifestation needs a decision. Sometimes you just say to yourself, "Wow, it'd be nice to have another $10k sale today" and one comes in out of nowhere.

"This is how I manifest from *flow!*" I'll hear women say.

Surprise manifestations are nice, but when it's time to call things in predictably and consistently – which is usually how we want our money manifestations to go down – a decision is *required*.

When you are "one foot in – one foot out," you're impressing that waffly energy on the Field. How can it respond back with what you want when the energy put in is scattered, unclear, half-hearted?

Answer: it can't. Which is why the longer you choose to hold back from claiming the money, opportunities, clients, and abundance that is already here, the more you delay its actual arrival.

The great news is, the opposite is also true. When you have absolute clarity and certainty, your good can show up immediately – sometimes even in an instant.

I have *so* many stories of this throughout my life and business. Most recent being, our "cute little four-story farmhouse" in the middle of Portland.

My husband and I had been in the waiting game for a house for years. Years. We both had a long list of requirements. So long, in fact, that we doubted many times whether it was even possible to find a house that fit them all.

Then, one day, on Memorial Day weekend in 2020 (two months into the COVID-19 lockdown), I got the hit. *It's time to get the house now. Get the house now!*

"Okay," I shrugged. I called up Redfin.

The first house on the list looked familiar. I sent it over to my husband, Leland.

He laughed, "You sent me this listing a year ago."

I searched my email, and sure enough, there it was. "I think this place might work for us," I had said.

Who knows why we didn't take the house back then. We probably ruled it out, considering all those criteria. This time, though, I made an immediate appointment.

We went to see it the next day and made an offer. It ticked *every* box on the list.

THERE IS MORE THAN ENOUGH FOR YOU

In *The Science of Getting Rich*, Wallace Wattles says something kind of wild.

"The Universe is more eager for you to have what you want than you are to have it."

I believe it's because our brains are naturally set up to look for, and confirm, situations of lack. Whether it was your mom budgeting your family's grocery bill to the penny, or your dad having to work extra hours, or you just saw too many newscasts about children living in poverty, or *you* were the one growing up in poverty... as children, we are conditioned to the state of "lack," in myriad ways, pretty much since birth.

It doesn't have to be this way. The Law reminds us that circumstances of lack are created by the lack programming in our minds, coupled with good old-fashioned greed, fear, and lust for power.

To activate abundance and call in pretty much any amount of money that is a true Desire of the heart, we must reject the programming and align with Truth. Then, take action from *that* place. And stay steadfast in the place of "abundance just is, there is no lack, only lack circumstances" no matter what.

It's not easy. But fortunes have been made with this one principle alone.

What you Desire and require *has* to be in your world already. Period.

It is Law.

6

THE CONFIDENCE STANDARD

A s I mentioned in Chapter 2, years ago, I was a part of the comics industry. Or maybe not quite a part of. I hung on, let's say. I tried to break in. I never quite made it, mostly because it wasn't what I was really meant to be doing.

Nonetheless, that time in my life was one of the best. The comics industry and the people in it were really good to me. One of those people was a woman named Kelly Sue.

These days, Kelly Sue is a master storyteller and a very accomplished and well-known writer both in and out of the comics industry. Back then, though, we were just two women making our way, hanging out in New York and living a creative life.

At the time, I thought that writing comics was *the*

thing. What could be cooler than writing comics and getting *paid* for it? Except maybe drawing comics. So, I threw myself into "breaking in" with the zeal of, well, every other would-be writer trying to break in.

I was crazy about stories and storytelling. So naturally I was filled with self-doubt.

I was also crazy about – wait for it – boys. Far from being a cabal of nerds, the comics industry has some hot ones. I flirted with as many of them as I could – when I wasn't wracked with self-doubt, that is.

One of them, Brian, truly captivated my attention.

(Yes! This is a story about a real-life crush with the same name as our nickname for the "doubting brain!" Oh, the irony! But I don't have the heart to change his name for the purposes of this book. It just doesn't feel right. My apologies, dear reader, for the possible confusion.)

Hailing from Vermont and lured to New York City by art school, Brian wrote and drew comics by night and worked as a designer at a video game company by day. Brian had a thing for bike couriers, Asian cinema, and New York City. His comics about teenagers and New York under siege got him lots of attention; he very quickly became an indie darling.

On weekends, we'd all go to Ace Bar in the East Village and drink and laugh and share projects and I'd ogle and get lost in the crowd and not say very much.

But Brian – Brian was onto me. I had a terrible crush on him. What's more, I had a crush on what he did. Doubt on overdrive. So bad that I could barely make a move. Despite the fact that he was flirting with me and sending me emails about, well, never mind.

Back at Kelly Sue's apartment, I'd let it all out. I would rant about how insecure I felt and I-don't-know-if-he-likes-me and I-don't-know-if-I-have-what-it-takes and dear-god-am-I-cool-enough.

One night, after a particularly long self-doubt tirade ("what if this" and "what if that" and … and … and), Kelly Sue sighed a small sigh and turned to me.

"Elizabeth, you don't really get how cool you really are, do you?"

It wasn't the first time I'd heard this from a friend. Which is a little weird. I mean, who says that to someone?

Apparently, a lot of people – as evidenced by the number of my clients who, when I tell this story, share that they've heard the same thing. And the fact that I'd heard it from at least two other friends during that couple-year span of New York life.

Now, you may not have ever had someone say, "Goddess, you just don't *get* how cool you really are, do you?"

But I'm thinking you might be able to relate to this, yeah?

Because here's the thing: We've all experienced doubt and insecurity. Hello, being human. For me, both trying to break into the comics industry and trying to get through grad school triggered massive doubt.

For example, grad school in computer science is friggin' hard. Once the smartest girl in the room, I quickly found myself wayyy out of my depths in subjects like operating system design, foundational algorithms, and – wait for it – compiler construction.

Meanwhile, over in the creative hotbed that is the comics industry, I was running into the pesky upper limits that come with being a stifled creative.

And then there was Brian. (The guy, in this case, not the lying brain.)

Doubt happens. It was triggered for me something fierce back then and many times since.

Here's the kicker, though:

Have you noticed something?

High-performing women *love* to go on and on about how we're not enough.

And sure, we've got the conditioning and the patterning and the systems of oppression that we're all swimming in, and the patriarchal programming and let's not forget the core belief of *lack* and not enough that's baked into the fabric of our existence and all, and I could go on. Sure, all of that will create some doubt and illusion-of-not-enough-ness.

And yet. Yet.

I would put it to you, dear reader, especially the women reading this, because most of our clients are women, that secretly, in our heart of hearts, we know the truth.

Oh, yes. We know the truth that we've freaking got it going on. And that one does not really have to look all that far to uncover the got-it-going-on-ness that we collectively have.

And we know it.

You just don't get how cool you really are, do you, Elizabeth?

Uh, actually, I kind of do.

Oh, wait… yes I do.

So, when am I going to *choose* to stop energizing *doubt* and exude confidence? Because my awesomeness just is. Your awesomeness just is.

When are we going to stop energizing doubt and start energizing what's real?

What's real is you've got it going on.

What's real is that you *already* have mad skills, you've *already* created success, your clients have already rocked it out on your watch.

So, what the hell, Goddess? When are you gonna make up your mind that your awesomeness just is?

This is the essence of the Confidence Standard.

YOUR AWESOMENESS JUST IS

The Confidence Standard is holding the truth that your awesomeness just is. You've already got it going on and that's just how it is.

Now, at this point I should tell you that out of all of the Standards you will discover in this book, hands down, the Confidence Standard is the one that I hear about the most. It's the one that "everyone" said is the most impactful for them.

Kinda interesting, isn't it?

I'll admit that at first, I didn't quite get it. Confidence, what gives? Don't we all have it?

Yes and no. Whether or not we "have confidence" really only scratches the surface of what holding Confidence as Standard really does.

Regardless of whether we have confidence, we all 100 percent absolutely, positively have *doubt*. The Confidence Standard is an active release of the unsupportive engagement with the Ultimate Manifestation Killer: doubt.

When we activate the Confidence Standard – that is, when we hold Confidence as something that just is – we activate a new way of be-ing that truly has the potential to change everything.

Old way: something comes into your field, triggers doubt, and you fall right into it.

New way: something comes into your field, triggers doubt, and you move right on. Align with Truth and move on.

We all have doubts and fears. Every one of us.

A big part of making your income leap, creating your cash infusion, and ultimately collapsing time to seven-figures in two years or less is that *ultimately*, at a certain point, you have to just stop energizing doubt and fear and *engage* the Truth.

CONFIDENCE AND UNIVERSAL LAW

Let's go back to the Laws for a moment.

One, the Laws tell us that what you energize manifests. Whatever you direct your attention and energy to, in an ongoing way, is what's going to show up. (You've heard this as "what you focus on expands" and many other ways.)

Two, the Law of Polarity, which we talked about at great length in the last chapter, basically says: You cannot have a Desire for a thing without the way for it to be made manifest to also be present.

It's already here. It's already done.

So, basically, the Laws say, whatever the Desires of your heart are, you can have them. It's already here, and when you direct your focus and take aligned action, you can have them. The way we work with Law is by aligning with them. When we align with Law, we connect to the bigger fabric of all that is.

Also? Like natural laws like the Law of Gravity, Universal Law is always working. And we are always working with it, whether we have conscious awareness of it or not.

So, what happens when you introduce doubt and energize doubt?

DOUBT: THE ULTIMATE MANIFESTATION KILLER

When you say you're going to manifest something and then introduce doubt, what happens?

Well, in essence you are going directly against the Law. You are also falling out of harmony with the bigger fabric of all that is. And when we do that, we create separation.

Therefore – and here's the radical bit – when we energize doubts and fears (which, I don't have to tell you, we're usually doing all day long, consciously and unconsciously), there is literally no way we can be energizing what we actually want.

Unfortunately, you can't be focused on two things at the same time. It's just not how the brain operates. So, when you energize doubt, you send your energy in a direction that is in the opposite of what you want, and naturally, it is going to create the opposite of desired results.

Truth: Thou Art Goddess. You are a Divine be-ing.

Truth: It's already here.

Truth: What you direct your energy to manifests.

But when you introduce doubt, and engage with doubt, you create a break in *all of that*. You create separation from your Divine Nature.

Remember this quote from Peter Reding?

"There is only one problem, and that is separation. There is only one solution, and that is connection."

We kinda all know this.

The first thought that creates separation is *doubt*.

And separation from your Divine Nature translates into massive, massive delays in manifestation.

And really, you only have to look to your own experience to know this is true, right? I mean, have you ever created something easy-peasy, lemon-squeezy while you were hung up in doubt?

Think of a bold goal you have. For fun, let's make it about money.

Where are you doubting? That's where you're creating delays.

Now, of course you're a human being! You're going to doubt! Right?

The practice, though, as a magician, is to see the Truth. Seeing the Truth means blocking out doubt.

We want to do this with radical acceptance so we're not creating more resistance.

And you don't need to be perfect. It is a *practice*. It's going to be there, so you might as well not fight it. You just don't let it drive the car.

What this means, though, in practice, is that you act as if your success is 100 percent ensured. Period.

CUTTING OUT THE BULLSHIT – WHICH IS DOUBT

This is one of those "cut the nonsense" Standards. Because being anything less than 100 percent confident in your you-ness is nonsense. Like, there are *zero* other alternatives or options. You know?

Now I know this is edgy. I can feel some of my dear readers going "!!!!" on the inside or wanting to throttle me a little or maybe going, "Don't put me in a box!"

To which I say, don't turn this into a power or authority struggle within yourself or with me as an "authority figure" (spoiler alert: I'm not one) or "authority figures" in the past.

Letting go of doubt isn't a "have to."

We let go of doubt because, if you think about it, it's the only thing that actually *makes sense*.

We're going to talk about this even more in the next chapter, with the Expectation Standard. Because they are two halves of the same thing. (Confidence Standard: confidence in yourself. Expectation Standard: confidence in others and 100 percent expectation in Creative Substance to deliver.)

PRACTICAL APPLICATION #1: WORKING WITH YOUR CLIENTS TO GET RESULTS

Imagine, if you will, that you've just signed up with a new transformational leader – a new coach, healer, hypnotherapist, practitioner, or similar.

You show up for that first session. You're excited, and a little nervous. And yes, part of you is wondering, "Did I make a good decision?"

Then, the first thing your coach says is, "I dunno, those are some big goals you've got there. Oh, hell, I'm not really sure I can help you get the results you're looking for."

Or, "Hm, maybe this isn't going to work out. I hear that you're making more money than me. That's an automatic disqualification. Nope, no way I can help you."

Man, that would suck, wouldn't it?

And yet, isn't that what Leaders do all the time? Doubt (within themselves) that they can actually deliver the result?

And this especially applies to high-performing, already-successful, loads-of-experience, rock star women with a list of rock star clients a mile long.

Reading it now, you can see that it's pure nonsense.

Well, the Confidence Standard is where we stop engaging in the nonsense. The Confidence Standard is where we stop energizing "Can I really deliver?" and instead boldly claim and stand by what you know you can and do deliver, and have delivered a zillion times already.

It sounds almost crazy to even paint this picture. It's like, do people really act this way?

But it happens all the time. Subconsciously, which is why it's so challenging to recognize in everyday life.

This kind of doubting that you can deliver is a big problem. Because not only is confidence a hell of a lot more fun than doubting yourself, but it's also a key aspect of getting your clients results.

Simply put, your clients want – and are paying for – your confidence, not only in them (that's the next Standard) but also in yourself.

And again – if we think about it – why on earth would anything else be accurate or true? Why would any of us hire someone, consciously, when they don't have confidence?

If you paid a heart surgeon a ton of money, and then as they were about to put you under, you hear them saying, "Oh, shit, not sure I can pull this off today, I got cut off on the freeway and that always messes with me" – that'd be a little bit concerning, no?

Another aspect of leveraging confidence to

increase your clients' results is *their* confidence in *themselves*.

When someone has just hired us, they're in a vulnerable place. They have tried to solve their problem before and failed. It should come as no big shocker that they are *not* necessarily confident in their ability to solve the problem. Most of the time, they don't actually believe they can do it.

Therefore, one of the things they're paying for is your confidence in *them*, which begins with your confidence in *you*.

(Again, think about it – why would you have confidence in them if you had no confidence in you? Makes no sense whatsoever.)

Energy follows energy. Your clients are always going to follow your lead. So why not make it easy for them and you?! (Man, shizz is hard enough!)

So, here's an instant hack to help your clients get better results: be confident in what you do and in what you're doing with them, even when there are some wobbles.

You can be with the wobbles *and* energize confidence. Clients, in turn, will follow your lead.

When you are confident – what happens? Their vibration shifts. They are energizing confidence and *expectation* (the secret sauce we'll talk about in the next chapter).

If all you did was up your confidence in your programs, they would get even better results.

How do we cultivate confidence? Look at the *facts*.

After having her first baby and taking an extra-long maternity leave, our client Penelope Jane Smith quickly ramped her business back up to six figures by offering one-to-one VIP coaching packages to help entrepreneurial women create a strategy for complete financial independence in five years or less.

Immediately, she hit a ceiling because she ran out of time that she could sell. "I was in danger of hating my life and my business if I took on any more clients," Penelope said.

Despite being one of the premier experts in creating financial freedom (Penelope created her first real estate empire in her mid-twenties), she was keeping this aspect of her work on the down low. She wanted to offer her Highest Level Work, but she held back because she was afraid.

"What if I offer what I *really* want to offer... and nobody signs up?"

In our work together, Penelope activated the Confidence Standard. And that's when she saw the facts on the ground.

Mentors – *many* mentors – with far less experience, were selling their financial freedom packages for far more money.

"It blew my mind to see many people in my industry proclaiming how amazing they were and charging $25,000 to $100,000, even though they didn't have as much experience as I do or offer as much value.

"I have a weird tendency to think that everyone knows what I know, but the truth is that after investing $500,000 and twenty years of my life into my education so far, I've become the best in the world at what I do. There are very, very few people on the planet who can match the breadth and depth of my experience in this area."

Now, you might not have invested twenty years of your life and 500 g's to know what you know.

But you know what?

I'd bet a milkshake that you have. Or it's quite close.

And when you look at the facts, it's like… why are you discounting, again?

Years ago, one of the very first coaching exercises I ever created was "The List of Evidence."

It's very simple – in fact, after you read what I'm about to share, I encourage you to put the book down, and do it. Here it is.

Take out a fresh sheet of paper and make a list of everything that has contributed to the value of your work. Be sure to include:

- Trainings and apprenticeships
- Schooling, degrees, etc.
- Life experiences
- Natural talents and skills

- Skills and talents you've honed & developed over time
- Programs you've created
- Books you've written
- Positions you've held
- People you've helped and specific results they've achieved
- What clients and other people in your life value about you
- What you value and appreciate about yourself
- Anything else that you want to put down!

Once you have your list, allow yourself some quiet time to go into a meditative state.

Then read the list out loud, slowly and carefully, letting every word sink in.

Go ahead. Do it now. I'll wait.

Annnd… welcome back.

Now, what were you saying?

Something about "not being good enough" to reach out to that potential client, create that offer you really want to go for or charge $50k for one-on-one work with you?

PRACTICAL APPLICATION #2: YOUR FEES

Years ago, a mentor said to me, "Elizabeth, your fee reflects your confidence in your skill set." It's very true.

Brace yourself before you read the next sentence because what I'm about to tell you might blow your mind.

The only difference between someone charging $1k and $20k for the transformation is energy, confidence, and what they are embodying.

Remember that exercise I just had you do? That List of Evidence?

Guess what? All of that is worth something. All those things you've done in your life are worth something. Like, a lot of something.

It is really worth something to *be* the being who has created the results you have created.

And it's worth something to have gone through what it took to get there.

Also? For clients to really change, they must commit. To commit, they must have some skin in the game. Nobody at seven figures already goes "all in" on a $297 program. And they will absolutely blow you off and *not* take you seriously if you're hanging out charging low fees that do not reflect what you're rocking.

Higher fees are part of your transformational chops.

From this perspective, you actually *need* to charge

your clients more. The fact that you've done the work on yourself to make your ability to do what you do even possible.

Again, I'll use myself as an example. About two years after my daughter was born, my husband and I reached a crisis point in our marriage. (Want to see what a marriage is really made of? Have children!)

Both of us bumped up against core patterning and childhood trauma that were keeping our next level of Divinity from emerging.

Let's not mince words here. We were headed for divorce, or passing those patterns on to our daughter. So together, we stepped into therapy, NLP – a cauldron of transformation. The shit was *intense*. There were many, many days when I thought we weren't going to make it.

But we did make it. And we're still going strong. And I was forever changed.

The work we did together *directly* impacted my business. Because all of those patterns I was playing out with him were getting played out with my clients as well.

If you look at me now versus me then – it's like night and day. Doing that work is in no small part what qualifies me to do what I do, and get paid richly for.

The same is true for you.

These days, after so many years and all that I've

done, I refuse to accept any idea that I can't deliver, and that our clients can't receive.

Your fee reflects your confidence in *everything*.

You *earned* the right to be confident from all the work you've done.

Then you earn the right to be confident from all the work you will do.

How many people actually do the shizzle that we do, in order to be able to do what we do? Very few.

It's "normal" in the transformation industry to "do the work" (although a lot of that is bypass – I don't say that from a judging place).

So we think it's normal and it's worth nothing.

It's *not* normal. And it's worth a *lot*.

As with all the Standards, when we activate the Confidence Standard, we move from negotiating with ourselves and "can I or can't I?" to "this just is."

We use the Confidence Standard by holding the space where you claim what you know, you claim what you can deliver, you claim confidence in them (which leads to the Expectation Standard, the next standard).

Confidence is just something you accept and allow.

You start to see what the lack of it is – that is, just a way to stay the same – doubt, fear, critter brain doing its thing, safety patterning, or family loyalty patterning.

The Confidence Standard is where you say, "I no longer accept or believe that."

Your ability to deliver *just is*. It is what it is. It already exists.

Like anything, we can align with the Truth or choose to align with the illusion.

The Confidence Standard is where you choose to align with what you already know you can do.

THIS IS NOT A PARADOX

I said above that we earn confidence. I also said here we accept and allow confidence. This sounds like a paradox, but it isn't.

We *accept* the fact that we have got it going on, we *allow* what follows from that, and we *continue* to build on that. We continue to work on and build confidence.

And *count* your successes along the way, instead of discounting them. Train your brain rather than allow it to push you around.

HOW TO USE THE CONFIDENCE STANDARD

In order to use the Confidence Standard, we have to do two things.

One is to consciously *grow* confidence.

Grow it: "This is a thing that exists within me, that I am constantly growing."

And *guard* it. Not from a place of fear and doubt, but from a place of being the steward.

"I am the steward of my business, the steward of my energy, what I'm here to do, and who I help."

"I take care of me, so I'm going to guard my confidence – my perception of Truth rather than collective consciousness."

Because your awesomeness just is.

Nothing to do, shift, fix, or prove.

It just is. And it is, right now.

THE EXPECTATION STANDARD

Ryan Moran is one of my favorite mentors in the online space. As the creator / founder of Capitalism.com, Ryan mentors ecommerce business owners to seven figures and then to make seven-figure exits.

Ryan lives in Austin, a city known for its thriving community of young entrepreneurs. On a call, I heard him tell a story about a personal trainer, of all things.

Ryan went looking for a personal trainer shortly after he moved to Austin. Personal trainers not being all that hard to come by, he found one that he liked and dove into blasting away the extra padding that had settled in after a few too many "Wine with Wyan" Facebook Lives for the Capitalism.com community.

So far, so good, no big deal. Then he heard about "The Guy."

"The Guy" was the trainer that *everyone* was hiring – all his ultra-successful millionaire entrepreneur friends. They were all rocking it, successful in his program, and getting the results.

There was just one thing about "The Guy," though. While most trainers charged $80 - $100 bucks for a single session, "The Guy" charged $5,000 for ninety days.

$5,000 for a personal trainer? WTF? Must be... um, good?

So he ponies up $5,000 and hires the guy.

The Guy is like, "Here's what's going to happen. This, this, and this."

Ryan thinks, "Wow. I'm really gonna do it. This extra weight is going to come off, and I'm gonna be shredded."

And The Guy just confirms matter-of-factly. "Yep."

What happened next was quite predictable. The weight came off, and Ryan got shredded.

Now here's the thing:

Along the way, Ryan had a few important realizations. The first was, wow, this guy is kinda like any other trainer, except he charges $5,000!

The other realization was: *Wow, because I paid $5,000, I'm showing up entirely differently than I would have for "just another" trainer.*

Finally, he realized that "The Guy" expected his clients to succeed and set expectations as such.

Nothing impossible to meet or "off the chicken," but he was clear: you're going to come in here and do the thing, and you're going to win.

And his clients won. Consistently.

THE EXPECTATION STANDARD: EXPECTING WHAT YOU WANT – AND GETTING IT

In the previous chapter, we took a deep dive into the power of Confidence – where you walk about the world knowing that your awesomeness just is and claim what you know, what you're capable of, and what you can deliver. And you stop telling yourself LIES about yourself, what you're capable of, and what you already deliver.

Instead of buying into the illusion that "you can't do it," "you'll never do it," "you suck," or "why are you doing this in the first place again," you choose confidence. You're already awesome and that's just how it is.

With the Expectation Standard, we hold the same fierce, non-negotiable, no-messing-around energy. Only this time, our confidence is in *others* and Creative Substance to deliver. This time, we hold the 100 percent expectation in other people to show up and rock it out, and the 100 percent expectation that Creative Substance (Source, God / Goddess, the Field) will deliver.

You expect your clients to succeed... and for yourself, you expect Creative Life Force Energy or Creative Substance to deliver exactly what you Desire.

You *expect* amazingness, and you *get it.*

Now, it should go without saying that this is not an ego-driven, attempt-to-control kind of expectation. I mean, you're not the teacher expecting your clients to do their work to please you. Nor are you engaging in entitled demanding of the world and Creative Substance like a spoiled little kid!

As always, the Expectation Standard activates the energy of "this just is."

Your clients are Divine. They are capable of great things. They are capable of rocking it. They just will, because why on earth would they not?

Similarly, when you hold the Expectation Standard, it's because *you* know how the Universe works. You know that there are Universal Laws that govern creation and outcomes and that they work 100 percent of the time when used properly. Period. No exceptions. (Because gravity always works, doesn't it?)

You expect money. You expect joy. You absolutely expect great things to be delivered to you when you are operating from your Highest Level.

You expect best of the best of the best clients to show up. You expect them to pay large amounts of money without drama. You expect them to be happy about it. You're overjoyed, because you know who they are! You expect them to rock it out, and of course they do.

Because this just is.

THE BUSTED ASSUMPTION THAT KEEPS EVERYONE STUCK

Have you ever said to yourself, "I'll believe it when I see it?"

You'll believe that the clients are there when you can actually see them. You'll believe the money is there when it shows up in your bank account. You'll believe that you can make that leap from $200k to seven figures in eighteen months when you actually *do* it.

This is a very natural line of thinking. This is Brian at his finest.

Unfortunately, it doesn't work that way. Instead, Creative Substance (the Thinking Stuff from Which All Things Are Made, the Field of All Potentialities, Source Energy, The Source of All Things) works more like this:

Expect to see it, then you can have it.

This goes for you, and it goes for your clients, too.

Want fast results? Want to collapse time to seven figures in two years or less? Expectation is your secret sauce.

The reason why you're not attracting the clients you want or getting the results you want is somewhere along the line energetically, there is a part of you that has decided that you can't have that.

You *get* the results you expect. And if they aren't showing up yet, that's feedback for you, and you keep expecting as you course correct and you keep expecting until you get it.

Don't quite believe me? Don't quite believe that this works every time? Let's go back to the Laws....

WHAT YOU ENERGIZE, MANIFESTS, REDUX

If you're into Law of Attraction at all – if you've ever watched The Secret or anything like it – then you've heard things like "your thoughts create your reality." Indeed, you've very likely seen this working in your own life: what you think about on a regular basis is what keeps showing up.

What this truism is really speaking to is energy and the direction of it. As we've discussed, everything is made up of energy, and in one sense, what are thoughts but packets of energy with structure and meaning?

Energy comes in so many forms, so why be limited by thoughts?

That is why we say in Feminine Magic®: what you energize, manifests. What you send energy toward (or what you are *energizing*) consistently and long term, is what's going to show up.

Frankly, that in and of itself is pretty darned cool.

Just for fun and just because we can, let's take a minute and remember why that is so awesome. Oh, the co-creative power we wield, just by directing our energy!

Even more cool?

It really doesn't take a lot to send energy in the right direction. Why? Because energy always follows intent.

I know I just dashed that off up there, but this really is one of the magician's secrets of the ages, one of those things they wouldn't teach you in mystery school until you've demonstrated that you can handle the ramifications. (Of course, this is always happening anyway, without this knowledge; in that case, it is going toward unconscious patterns and programs that keep the status quo – in other words, it's not going to rock any boats.)

Energy always follows intent. Always.

Therefore, if you *expect* something, like results for your clients, results for you, or whatever, you are essentially using intention in the right way – which is to direct energy very consciously and purposefully.

The personal trainer in the previous story charged $5,000 – which is a lot for a personal trainer. He expected a lot of his clients, and his clients expected him to be fabulous, because he charged so much. Both expectations came true.

Expectation is quite different from the "normal" way people set intentions, which is to "set it and forget it." There are times where that is useful, but 90 percent of the time it perpetuates the misunderstanding that you can just be in your normal way and you get what you want simply because you set your intention.

When you consciously direct energy through Expectation and then back that up by *being* the version of you for whom this is true, you're sending all the energy, all the time.

So, you can see, how from here on out, it's a very good idea to have extraordinary expectations for your clients, yourself, and the world. And how you set yourself up for success when you have expectations for others in your world (clients, team, family) and hold fast to them.

(This is not the same thing as being pie-in-the-sky la-la land when someone is treating you badly. Though it is quite interesting and fascinating how quickly we can turn around the pattern of "others treating us badly" when we expect others to treat us well, and we back those expectations up with action.)

The Expectation Standard is where we get to stop looking at how things will go wrong and start expecting them to go *right* as a practice. We expect clients to rock it out, and we expect them – and us! – to get everything we truly want and apply ourselves to. And we usually do it in a fraction of the time. Because – you guessed it – it just *is*.

So, what expectations should we have, when

we're wanting to collapse time and leap to seven figures (or a really big number) in two years or less?

You get to decide, but as you might imagine, there are a few that I highly recommend if you want to make a big impact.

PRACTICAL APPLICATION #1: EXPECT YOUR CLIENTS TO BE THERE AND EXPECT THEM TO SUCCEED

In my experience, there is no better way to speed up the results of client attraction than to use the Expectation Standard.

First, expect that your Next Level clients are there. (Hint: by Law, they are always there. Always.)

Next, expect that they will become visible to you when you show up with the Frequency (ways of being) that attracts them. (Hint: by Law, they always will.)

Expect those Next Level clients to say *yes* to your offers, step in, and happily pay you scads of money.

And finally, expect them to succeed.

There's an interesting phenomenon in the "transformation space" when it comes to the Charging of Big Fees.

First of all, everyone wants to do it. Over the past fifteen years, "high-end" fees have become the norm. There was a time when they were not the norm – charging by the hour was the norm. Then, someone figured out to price based on value, not by the hour. Hundreds of thousands of Leaders started making a lot more money and freeing up a lot of time.

Everyone loves big fees, and big fees are the norm, but (of course) Law of Polarity being what it is, we have the downside as well as the upside. Occasionally, something bad will happen. Peeps get burned by big fees.

When peeps get burned by big fees, suddenly, the bellyaching about big fees comes out. And we collectively forget that, for your Next Level Clients, investing the big bucks means expecting to succeed!

When Ryan paid his trainer $5,000, he had a little "Wow, this is expensive" followed immediately by "Wow, this guy must be good" followed by "Wow, if the guy is that good, then surely I will win."

His trainer set up the expectation that he would succeed, too. "Do this, this, this, and this."

Lo and behold, Ryan followed the trainer's lead and succeeded!

Energy follows intent. What happens when you expect your clients to succeed?

Chances are, they will.

It's helpful to remember here that energy follows energy – your clients are *always* following your lead. So, if you're all up in your wiggly boos about them getting results, guess what? They are going to pick up on that unconsciously and bring their energy down. (If that sounds like a killjoy, it is.).

Expect to succeed. Because here's something else you might not realize.

When clients pay big chunks of money , your expectation that they will succeed is what they are paying for – whether they know that or not. They are *investing* in your belief in them because they don't have that belief all locked up tight themselves.

Note that this is not about giving them a ton of stuff. Or extra. It's about telling them what you expect! And then expecting them to succeed because they're awesome and they can do it.

One of those tools you have for them to win is being very clear on what you expect. Tell your clients how to show up, in no uncertain terms.

Years ago, I worked with a weight-loss coach named Cristy "Code Red" Nickel. Cristy is a former boxer, and when I took my first look at her, with her chiseled body, brightly colored mohawk, and "take no prisoners" expression, I was part thrilled (OMG the results are going to be amazing!) and part terrified (this woman is going to kick my ass).

After doing her initial thirty-day starter program, I ponied up the big bucks ($997 back then) for her custom program, where she worked out all your numbers: macros, ounces of water to drink every day, and so on.

Cristy works with a more mainstream, non-entrepreneurial clientele. To them, $997 is a lot. They're not what would be considered "high-end" or "elite" clients by the online coaching industry. And yet Cristy treats everyone like the Goddess or Adonis they already are. She also holds them to very high standards.

When my program arrived in the mail, I could barely contain myself as I called up the YouTube video of Cristy walking me through the program.

"Here's what you can expect," the video began. "We'll also go over my expectations of you as one of my clients."

Here's what's on the food list. Here's what's not on the foods list. Here are the supplements you need to be taking. Here's the amount of water you need to be drinking. Yes, you will drink that amount of water every day, no exceptions. Here's the amount of sleep you need to be getting. Do not go less than the required amount of sleep. Here's when you need to stop eating for the day. Of course, there is no snacking.

At the end of the video, she looked me straight in the eye. "Now you know what's expected. Most of all, I expect compliance."

Over the top? Maybe. Hardcore? Definitely. What I know for sure is that Cristy has legions of raving fans, men and women of all ages and all walks of life, who have used her program to take the weight off and succeeded, when nothing else worked. Go to one of Cristy's events and don't be surprised if it's like you're in the room with Robert Plant. Or Justin

Bieber. Or Billie Eilish. Or – if you're me – Tori Amos.

Cristy's clients gush over her. A meeting is a cathartic experience, complete with all the feels. And they keep paying her and paying her and paying her.

Cristy's clients are not "high-end" or "elite" by coaching industry standards. They go to nine-to-five jobs and play with their grandkids on weekends. They watch Netflix at night with their husbands and meal prep on Sundays. ("Normal" stuff! Gasp!)

And yet Cristy expects greatness. She expects the extraordinary. She doesn't bring her energy down to where she thinks they are or where they think they are. She lifts her energy up. She sets a clear expectation. And she gets it.

Truthfully, my inner "Don't tell me what to do, Mohawk Lady" was on fire during that video. But you know what? I knew exactly what was expected. There was zero ambiguity.

Also, it was made entirely clear that it was 100 percent on me if I didn't do what she asked.

Many transformational leaders experience blame shifting – clients lobbing the blame back on them for their lack of results. This is a huge cause of frustration and Inner Friction. What Leaders forget, though, is the reason all of this blame shifting usually comes about is because there was not a clear expectation set in the first place.

Instead, many Leaders engage in the game of "I

work with other Leaders who lead themselves." They should know. They should do. We shouldn't "have to" babysit or tell people what to do.

It's great in theory. What I've found, though, is that even high-performing leaders are just like other humble humans: they hit their resistance and sometimes have temper tantrums, and Brian (the brain) will want to shift it to you. Instead of being triggered by it, see it for what it is and set expectations up front.

PRACTICAL APPLICATION #2: EXPECT THAT YOUR PEOPLE WANT TO WIN

Maybe it's just me?

I can get judge-y with the "un-coachable" clients.

My brain zooms along at ninety miles per hour most of the time. And I like it that way, frankly. So when I'm sitting there hitting a clients' resistance and they keep throwing up excuse after excuse, I confess: I can get annoyed.

Years ago, in my masters-level NLP training, I watched my trainer take one of the demo clients through a similar pattern of resistance.

She kept lobbing out reframes, and they were still in the "waffle" zone.

I raised my hand:

"What if, deep down, your client just doesn't *want* to change?"

. . .

My trainer shot back:

"They *always want the change.*"

"But...," I protested.

"'But' nothing. They *always* want the change."

It hit me smack between the eyes, because as transformational leaders, we know she's right, yeah?

Clients don't waffle and waste your time on ninety-minute sales calls (or even fifteen-minute sales calls) because they "don't want to change."

It's because they hit their natural resistance. Brian gonna do what Brian gonna do.

And if you think about it, why would people consciously spend $5k to $50k on a program to work with you if part of them didn't want to change?

So, what is on *us* to do? Help them through it. Coach them through it. And energize that part of them that wants to win more than you're energizing the resistance.

Easy-peasy, nourishing, non-pushy way to do that? Expect that they want to win. Because they *do*.

We call people "un-coachable," and sometimes they are. People have to be willing to go past their stopping points.

Most of the time, they know this. Which is why they hired you!

Your people want to win. They are hiring you in no small part to believe in them.

So do it.

It's the same thing with your team. Ninety percent of the time, when a team member screws up, it's not because they're not capable or because they are trying to be a pain in the ass. It's because they were never really told what to do (by you) in the first place. And then we go bellyaching about how they screwed up and "Oh, they must not want to be there."

No. Like your clients, your team wants to win. So, assume that they want to win, and give them the tools to win. This is an assumption (and corresponding practice) that will set you free.

After all, why on *earth* would they be in your company if they didn't want to rock it out?

So, expect them to.

Now, does our every expectation "come true?"

It doesn't really matter. Who cares? There is no point *not* to do it. (More on this shortly.)

PRACTICAL APPLICATION #3: EXPECT YOURSELF TO WIN

One of my favorite energies of all time is the energy of "of course."

Of course, you're going to get the clients

Of course, you're going to fill the program, and so on.

You can be in a state of resistance, see it, and still go, "Of course."

Imagine that you're standing at the bottom of a hill with a big boulder. You have been tasked by God or Goddess to move the boulder up the hill (and your name isn't Sisyphus). You didn't ask for this, per se. (Except you probably did – remember, Divine Substance, Creative Life Force Energy, Source Energy, etc. – operates completely deductively, which means it can only give back to you in alignment with what you put in it.) But there you are, boulder "in hand," so to speak. At least you have a new pair of hiking boots on.

Now, I ask you, in that situation, which is going to be easier? Expecting to get that boulder up the hill, or expecting yourself to lose your footing and have said boulder roll back down to the bottom while you chase it, swearing and cursing?

Obviously, the former. Unfortunately, we are not conditioned for this. We are not conditioned for "of course I'll win, because, duh, of course, why would I not?"

We are conditioned for the latter. So we go forward in business, wanting to collapse time ever so much, only to hit on Inner Friction galore and to watch launches fail, programs not really fill, clients say no, the income goal not get met again, and, lo and behold, the boulders tumbling down all the hills.

As magicians, we get to turn this around. As

magicians, we know the power of expectation. We can expect to succeed – not because "oh no, what happens or what will I look like if I don't get it" – but rather because why on earth would we consciously choose anything but the Expectation Standard?

It doesn't make any sense.

MOVING OUT OF BE-ING "THE GURU"

Part of holding the Expectation Standard is activating the energy of Divine Equanimity: moving out of the "power over / power under" paradigm.

It's tempting to think that the Expectation Standard is about telling people what to do. But really, it's anything but.

When you hold the Expectation Standard, you let go of seeing people as "greater than" or "less than," or "above" or "below" you. Instead, you see people as creative be-ings making conscious choices (even when they're doing unconscious unsupportive stuff) and you hold that field of expectation.

And make no mistake – it is a field. Just as thoughts and mental images are things that actually exist... it *is* a field of expectation

The "field of infinite possibilities" is something you turn on. And it's crucial that you turn it on, through expectation. Or it's all too easy for the opposite of what you want to happen.

Because the first thought that causes separation is

doubt. And when we doubt, we cause massive, massive delays in manifestation.

Act as if your success is 100 percent ensured.

Expect your success to be 100 percent ensured.

Unless we're being chased by a woolly mammoth, there's little to no point in engaging fear. Similarly, there is zero point in doing something unless you expect to succeed.

Without 100 percent expectation that the thing will happen, you create separation. You end up impressing the Field with something *other* than expectation of success. You end up Impressing the Field with doubt.

Don't allow that. Don't settle for that.

"Settle" for your success being 100 percent ensured. Expect it.

And make that expectation something that just is.

8

THE DISCIPLINE STANDARD

A nd now, we come to the Standard that is simultaneously both the best ever and the one that everyone loves to hate.

I'm talking about the Discipline Standard!

Of course, I'm joking a little bit.

Or *am* I?

Hang with me. Because we're about to flip *discipline* on its head. I daresay you might even love discipline when we're done.

Because – as you'll see – while there are sexier Standards ("everything you want is already here," anyone?), the Discipline Standard is the most important one of all. Because it's the Discipline Standard that brings your dreams from imagination (the nonphysical planes) down to the 3D. The Discipline Standard is where shit gets done.

Or not.

7606108

All of the Standards are crucial. All are needed to create success. But the Discipline Standard is different from the rest.

The Discipline Standard is where we move from creating in the non-physical realm to the physical realm.

In other words, the Discipline Standard is where things get real. Literally.

OUTWITTING THE DEVIL

In 1938, Napoleon Hill wrote a "secret book."

I already mentioned Napoleon Hill and his best-known work *Think and Grow Rich*. You might have even read it a few times. Gleaned from the study of people who had amassed great personal fortunes (or so the story goes), *Think and Grow Rich* was first published in 1937 and has since become one of the highest-selling personal development books of all time.

Unlike its famous predecessor, *Outwitting the Devil* is *not* one of the highest-selling personal development books of all time. In fact, *Outwitting the Devil* was hidden away for years by his wife, and then by his successor's wife, until finally it was passed on to Don Green, CEO of the Napoleon Hill Foundation, and was finally published in 2011.

Outwitting the Devil shocked both women so much

that they refused to let it out of the attic, so to speak. The cause of the shock?

The Devil. Or "Your Majesty," as he is called in the book.

Who is the Devil? You might ask. Well, it's not the Devil like you or me.

In *Outwitting the Devil*, the Devil is the Devil that lives in our own minds. The Devil is the things that stop us, keep us from taking action, and ultimately halt us from fulfilling our potential and living our best life.

Simply put, the Devil in Napoleon Hill's book is resistance.

THE EVILS OF RESISTANCE

We've been talking about resistance throughout our whole journey together so far. We've also been stepping through a crash course in how we create our reality – a.k.a. how manifesting really works.

You are a Divine Be-ing living in a human body. Thou Art Goddess. You have a Divine Nature. You're living in a physical system. You have a Human Nature. That physical system and Human Nature have its own agenda! It has three brains, which all "duke it out" with competing priorities. The neocortex wants to expand, the critter brain wants to stay not dead, and the limbic brain wants to feel good and get along.

As a Divine Being, you create *instantaneously*. All planes, spaces, dimensions, times, levels of consciousness exist simultaneously. Create it on the non-physical, and in a very real sense, it is *done*.

This dual nature sets up resistance – that part of us that says "no, wait!" when another part of us goes "I want that!" The part of us that throws up all the doubt, fear, discomfort, and – let's be real – the digging in of the heels and the "I don't wanna."

Now, as we can see, resistance is a natural process. And, in my experience, setting something within ourselves up as "bad" or "wrong" rarely works out. So, to turn the Devil into a metaphor for resistance might seem a little hardcore.

Or is it?

Or is watering down resistance really the Devil speaking?

(To be clear – I am speaking of the Devil metaphorically here. The Devil may be part of your belief system. I mean no disrespect. The Devil is not part of my belief system, and for all I know, that might mean that you put the book down here and walk away. I'm not sure. For our intents and purposes, let's keep the Devil on the metaphorical level, where it is the most useful for this discussion.)

Here's the deal, dear reader, we can talk resistance down all we want – however we do it. We can say we're going to dance or play with it. We can say we're going to "make friends" with it.

Generally speaking, though, humans give in to resistance. The "I don't wanna" comes up, and we stop.

This is a *huge* problem because resistance kills your dreams.

That's the Truth, what is accurate, facts on the ground. Resistance kills dreams dead.

And unless you, dear reader, learn how to be able to take action in the face of it, it will kill your dreams dead, too.

There will be no seven-figure business. There will be no Next Level clients at high fees. There will be no full programs. There will be no collapsing time.

Most people just go on autopilot. Most people don't even know that that's what's going on.

They just know that they "don't wanna" or they're scared or whatever.

And so, they *don't*.

It's very natural. It's a biological process, even. But if we keep doing that, where do we end up? It's not with our Desires.

Going on autopilot is not freedom. It's very positive on the one hand. Our brains are amazing. We want to go on autopilot for a great deal of things.

But when we make a decision and then can't or won't follow through, we're in the conditioning. We're being ruled by our minds. We are essentially shackled.

We might not like to think of that as "the Devil," but hey, you've gotta admit that it's kinda apt.

Thankfully, though, we have the Discipline Standard. The Discipline Standard is where we turn all of this around.

EXERCISING YOUR POWER OF CHOICE, A.K.A. FOLLOW-THROUGH

Years ago, in some of my earliest magical training, I received a great definition of discipline.

"Discipline is your ability to give yourself a command and follow it."

To that end, I also received a bunch of somewhat weird exercises to promote discipline. One of them was to think of how you got to work (or school) every day – the same route you took every day. Then, give yourself a different way. You got extra points if you made it as out-of-the-way and inconvenient as possible. Then you were to use that way instead of your regular way for seven days straight.

Another one was to decide what *one* action you were going to take before going to bed that night. It had to be something that was a conscious choice to move your dreams forward. And then you didn't go to bed until you did it.

When we needed a break from all that, there was a simpler one: choose a spot on the wall, get up, walk over to the wall, touch the wall on that spot, and sit down again.

A few years ago, I stumbled on one of those hidden gems that makes you go "Goddess, bless the internet." Some intrepid soul had recorded a seminar from a Very Well-Known Personal Development Dude from the late nineties and posted it.

The Personal Development Dude tells the story of a group of initiates studying with their teacher in some remote country. (I'm paraphrasing a bit, as it's been ages since I heard this story, and I couldn't find it again. The message is just as sound as when I heard it years ago.)

Their teacher tells them to strip off all their clothes and go out in the middle of the woods (or maybe it was on top of a mountain) during the early morning hours for a very special task. The task was to dig a hole.

They all have to do it or they would get kicked out. So, they dug.

At the end the teacher says, "Okay, now fill it back up again."

"WTF is this for?" one of them asks.

Later, they find out the answer: to be able to take action while the mind is bellyaching at you. Until the mind becomes quiet.

Later on in the seminar, Personal Development Dude gives the attendees a simple exercise: take this slip of paper home, do a simple task, and when it was done, get the paper signed by someone they live with. He passes out the papers and everyone goes home.

The next day, he asks for peeps to present their signed papers. A few people had done the task and had the signed paper. A few others didn't do the task, but brought the paper back anyway. The rest had excuses.

"I forgot."

"I meant to, but I got pulled into the kids' homework."

"The dog ate it."

"What was the assignment again?"

"The point was to actually get the paper *signed*!" yells an emphatic Dude.

Excuses don't make your dreams real. "Forgetting" doesn't make your dreams real. Saying "I don't wanna" doesn't make your dreams real.

Giving yourself a command and following through makes dreams real.

This is your power of choice. This is the essence of Discipline.

THE DISCIPLINE STANDARD: WHEN YOUR POWER OF CHOICE IS SOMETHING THAT *JUST IS*

How would your life be different if you *fully* had and employed your power to choose?

If you could give yourself a command, then *follow*

it – regardless of fear, regardless of doubt, regardless of any physical sensations that you have in your body? (Yes, that too, all you somatic peoples.)

So, if you said, "Hey I'm going to eat nothing but whole foods, completely give up sugar," and it was done.

Or if you said, "Hey I'm going to save / tithe 10 percent of every dollar that comes in" and then it was done.

Or, I'm going to get up every day and write my daily email (or post) without fail / question, and then it was done.

Or, I'm going to make X amount of money in Y amount of time, and then it was done.

Or anything else you want to insert here…

How would life be different?

This isn't about deprivation, or being hard on yourself, or beating yourself up when you slip. It's not about restriction or taking away from.

The Discipline Standard is about *choice*. Choice means you add to rather than take away from.

Conditioning takes away your choice; discipline gives you back your choice.

Successful people have the ability to focus. They can also give themselves commands and then follow them. The command – which is just a choice, no judgment – becomes the rule of Law.

In other words, the choice you make determines your actions. Not how you feel, not your circumstances, not people in your family making fun of you, not what the clients you have had up until now will think, not all the people telling you no.

This is the essence of the Discipline Standard.

If you want to be at your Highest Level, at a certain point, you stop tolerating the "I don't wanna." Because "I don't wanna" is letting the ego mind run the show.

With the Discipline Standard, you do the thing, take the aligned action required.

And there's no charge around it – no inner battle with imaginary authority figures (which was my issue). There is only using your power of choice.

"I choose X, and it is because it is, and that's how it is."

We've been talking in this entire book about *not* engaging with doubt or fear. The Discipline Standard is where you do just that. When we activate the Discipline Standard, we make the choice and follow through.

THE PARADOX: IT IS BECAUSE YOU ARE!

Now here's the paradox. It can be hard to really *get*, so just hang in here and think.

One of the ways that people shoot themselves in the foot is thinking that they "have to" do things in a certain way in order to get the result. They forget that there are a zillion ways to create any goal. It's not that we don't choose a way – indeed, choosing the channel is very important. However, even when we choose a way, we are not thinking that's the only way. Because that takes all of the infinite possibilities for creating the outcome and collapses them into one.

We don't do those aligned actions because we think it's what's going to "get" money or "create the result."

You do the aligned actions because it's who you are. It's who you are be-ing.

Remember the Version of You Who Already Has It, from Chapter 2? Who *is* that person?

Thoughts and beliefs, emotions and feelings, energy patterns, physical body, environments, aligned actions – these things are just who you are.

If you *just are* the Transformational Leader who shows up in a certain way because you're committed to being a Transformational Leader and you're committed to your purpose.

Well, part of that is taking certain actions. You're just going to do it.

Not because you want to "get" money. But because you've *decided* that you are the leader and you're going to *be* that person and serve in a certain way and *live* your purpose.

It just is.

So – you message and create marketing (or have someone on your team do it) because that's just what you do.

You invite people because you invite people.

You eat however you eat because that's just how you, the transformational leader, does it.

You ask for the sale and charge a certain amount just because you do.

You make the choice because that's who you *be*. There is no room for anything else.

And – when you make a decision, and you give yourself a command, you follow through. Because you are a magician, and you know how to use your choice.

Now if you think about it, this is really *freeing*. Because if we tie our actions to the results we *think* we're gonna get, well, that just brings up more resistance.

"I don't wanna write my post today!"

If the action is tied to the outcome, you're in the energy of getting. Which puts you right back in the grasping and striving.

Instead, you are Doing the Thing because that's just what you do. That's who you *are*.

Not gonna lie – this one is difficult! Because the subconscious is sneaky!

But "Standard" doesn't mean "perfection." "Standard" means committing to it and then bringing yourself back to it. Which is all the Discipline Standard is anyway.

Also, notice that there's no "should-ing" with this one, either. I mean, how cool is that?

You're doing the thing because that's who you are and what you do. It just is.

The Discipline Standard is freedom.

"I PREFER NOT TO"

In eleventh grade English class, our teacher, Mr. Phippen had us read *Bartleby, the Scrivener* by Herman Melville.

Bartleby is hired by the unnamed elderly narrator as a third scrivener in the narrator's law firm. He's calm and collected, and hiring him is meant to calm down the other two uppity scriveners, who get grumpier by the day.

At first, Bartleby produces boatloads of quality work, but one day, when asked to help proofread a document, Bartleby answers with what soon becomes his response to every request.

"I would prefer not to."

Much has been made by critics, analysts, and high school juniors alike of the meaning of Bartleby's "I prefer not to" refrain. One theory is that it represents clinical depression – not that Melville (or anyone) was talking about clinical depression in 1853.

Despite all this, we start out thinking that Bartleby's "I prefer not to" is a refrain of autonomy – a pushing back against "the man," as 'twere.

And so, I can't help but think of Bartleby when there are simple, predictable steps to follow to get a desired outcome, and transformational leaders say, in essence, "I prefer not to!"

If you want to collapse time and create a seven-figure business in two years, you get to design that business however you want. This is one of our "un-rules."

However, just as none of us escape the laws of physics, none of us escape the rules of marketing, rules that are governed by human psychology that hasn't changed in over ten thousand years.

Of course, the "I prefer not to" is not about rules, or marketing, or even serving clients. It's about resistance.

"But it's not in alignment for me!" Leaders will say.

Of course, we want all the things to be in alignment for you. But in many cases, when our backs are against the wall of reality and we might have to do some things that are uncomfortable, "it's not in alignment" can sound, well, an awful lot like the parts of you that aren't really you.

We work with a lot of rebels and disruptors at 7-Figure Goddess®. Our clients want it their way and refuse to compromise on what's important. They also can't friggin' stand to be told what to do. Can you relate?

As someone who is really well-versed in the "I prefer not to," I've come to realize that the biggest authority figure I need to watch out for is Brian, my own mind, hopped up on resistance.

Do you "prefer not to," or is that resistance running the show?

Resistance kills your dreams.

Magicians, conscious co-creators who give themselves commands, follow them, and watch the whole world open up, get everything they Desire and more.

YOUR GREATEST POWER

The paradox here, of course, is that we go into our "I prefer not to" because we want to be at choice. We don't want to be told what to do, and we don't want to do the stuff that we don't want to do. And we think that clapping back with an "I prefer not to" is control, freedom, and being at choice.

But it isn't. It's digging us deeper and deeper into the hole of "no choice."

In Feminine Magic®, we have four "magic powers" to create anything we want. They are Perception, Energy, Faith, and Choice.

The greatest of these is your power to choose. Because it's only choice – a.k.a. action – that brings things from the imagination (non-physical) into the physical plane.

The Discipline Standard is consistently making choices in alignment with *who* you are be-ing, the version of you who already has the outcome. This is one of the ways that we move from the non-physical (our vision) to the physical (manifested in reality).

When we activate the Discipline Standard, and we take certain actions simply because it is how it is, because that's how you *be*, we activate our power to choose on steroids, as 'twere. We make actions automatic, w hich means we make our results automatic.

The Discipline Standard is also freeing because it's in the habits, actions, and environments that your dreams become not just achievable but also inevitable.

If you're disciplined about messaging because that's who you BE, if you consistently show up and serve at a High Level because that's who you BE, if you listen to your people and course correct and all of that – are you going to create your outcome?

Yes! Yes, you *are*.

INEVITABLE SUCCESS REQUIRES SACRIFICE?

There is a very important Universal Law that the Discipline Standard evokes: the Law of Sacrifice.

Raymond J. Holliwell talks about this law and calls it "the Law of Sacrifice" in his book *Working with the Law*. In essence, he points out that by Law, we must sacrifice something of a "lower nature" for something of a "higher nature."

Sounds scary, and our inner "don't tell me what to

do" can balk at this. The truth is, we are sacrificing all the time.

We sacrifice time with other people to spend time with the people we love.

We sacrifice our desire to eat sugar for releasing weight, a healthy body, and a long life.

We sacrifice Netflix time for reading books that will support our growth.

We sacrifice the "security" of a j-o-b for entrepreneurship!

"Sacrifice," as per the Law, simply means that we give up something "lower" for the thing that we say that we want – the "higher."

Unfortunately, when it comes to doing the hard stuff in our business, this is usually accompanied by a whole lot of resistance and bellyaching. What does that create? The Inner Friction that makes everything feel harder.

Instead, we can surrender to the sacrifice. Indeed, we can turn it into a sacrifice that has already happened, because we have already become the person who has done the damn thing and for whom it is no longer a so-called sacrifice. It just is.

Along the way, we can notice that this actually isn't such a big deal or so hard to do.

Why? Because resistance exists in the mind, nowhere else.

Resistance is a part of that Divine Nature–Human Nature inner conflict that gets played out by the three brains. (We covered this back in Chapter 4.)

It feels real, but it is not the Truth.

The Discipline Standard is Truth of Who You Are. You follow through on the choices made in support of your goals and dreams because that's just what you do.

The Discipline Standard makes those goals, dreams, collapsing time, and similar inevitable. That's the good news.

The bad news?

Without it, they will never happen at all.

What will you choose?

PRACTICAL APPLICATION: COLLAPSING TIME TO SEVEN FIGURES

By now, the practical application of the Discipline Standard should become clear.

We use the Discipline Standard to bring our goals and dreams from thought form to physical plane form. We make choices – a.k.a. we "do the stuff that's required" to make our dreams real.

And there's no avoiding it.

Deep down, just as we, as Leaders, are awesome, we *know*, as Leaders, that aligned action is a thing. We know this.

Resistance, and the actions of Brian to keep us in the same place, will trick us into believing otherwise. Which creates more Inner Friction that feels hard.

Resistance will hide the fact that at a certain point, there is nothing left to *do* but "do the do." Not what you *think* you have to do, but what is actually required to bring your dreams into full form.

A truly masterful magician leans into resistance instead of leaning away.

FACT: DO IT OR ELSE

Many years ago, I was in the throes of resistance. It was a couple of years into my business. I had a lot of "inner stuff" to work through – more than I knew at the time. And boy, was I all up in my "I don't want tos." So much so, that I created mountains of debt and was stalling in my business.

So, naturally, I went to a financial advisor to sort myself out.

This might seem like a weird move, but *this* financial advisor was special. Her name is Luna Jaffee, and she is local here in Portland. She is part coach, part advisor, and, of course, part ass-kicker, as I was to discover on that fateful day.

I was going over the laundry list of dreams – house, baby, and, of course, a ton of money in my business. "But we're six figures in debt," I moaned.

"Well, you need to do what it takes to get yourself out of debt," Luna said.

I can't remember exactly what I said, but it was something that essentially amounted to a whiny "I prefer not to."

Luna looked at me for a few seconds. Silence. Then she said:

"Look, Elizabeth, you're telling me you want a house, you want a baby, and you want your business to take off. Guess what? Those things *aren't* going to 'just happen.' They're not just going to magically show up on your doorstep someday. Your choice makes them happen. And if you don't start making the right choices, they simply aren't going to happen."

"Yeah, but I don't want to. It's going to take sooo long," I whined.

"Elizabeth. Your dreams will *not* happen."

That day was the day that allll of my previous magical training on Choice, Will, Discipline, and the power to choose finally locked into focus.

I didn't "want to" spend less. I didn't "want to" save money. I didn't "want to" sacrifice the pleasures of the now for the dreams of the future.

And neither do any of us!

The hard truth is without Discipline, without making conscious choices, our dreams simply won't happen.

FINAL TRUTH: THERE IS NOTHING TO "DO" BUT TAKE ALIGNED ACTION

Leaders get hung up on the "have to." But the truth is that only action can bring your dreams from thought form into reality.

Why, then, do we have so much resistance to action?

Because we engage in busywork. We do what we *think* we need to do. Even more often, we do what is comfortable rather than what is *required*.

If we wish to collapse time, to seven figures or anything else, it is a leadership move to realize that you get to let all that stuff go.

A simple fact of creating your reality is that there is never anything to "do." Your dream never, ever hinges on just "one thing," nor is there only one way to the destination.

(Okay, so maybe there is on rare occasion that one way. But it's rare. And really, I'm making this caveat for the sake of argument, not because it's actually true.)

There is never anything to "do." You don't "have to" run programs, attract clients, create a beautiful website, or make sales. Heck, you don't "have to" have a business at all!

But if you want a seven-figure business, there is always, *always* aligned action to take.

This can be another thing that is hard for overworked Leaders to swallow. Burnt out on action, Leaders want to skip action.

But there is *always* aligned action to take. Always.

With the Discipline Standard, we make it a part of our *be*-ing. We make the taking of aligned action simply a part of who we "be."

No Inner Friction, just taking the actions in front of us because we are choosing the thing.

And we watch those manifestations appear, right before our very eyes.

9

THE NO APOLOGIES STANDARD

E vening. Autumn Equinox.

The candles are flickering. The coven is gathered. I'm kneeling at the altar, consecrating the water and salt.

It's been a stressful week. Usually, Circle calms me down. But not this time.

This time, I'm leading, and I'm self-conscious. I flub the consecration words. The grains of salt fall off the tip of the blade and onto the table rather than into the water, where they are supposed to fall.

"Oops, sorry," I say.

My co-leader smiles at me. I can feel the rest of the group smiling, too. *What the hell? I've done this countless times.*

It is fall, the harvest season, but I am feeling anything but like we're having a good harvest. It's not just me. Everyone is feeling the pinch. Indeed, everything feels barren as there have been struggles at work, struggles at home, struggles that I am trying, and failing, to contain. They are leaking out, right here, in the middle of ritual.

The next blessing goes horribly wrong. I can't even remember the words. One of my sisters has to prompt me.

"Sorry!" I say.

Now it's time to cast the circle. Three times. *You can do this, Girl. This is like home to you. What is wrong with you?*

Except I trip. On a footstool that has been left out. WTF? Where did that come from? It's a small living room, Goddess. Chill.

The athame – the ritual blade – goes flying. I can see one of my coven mates duck for cover.

Oh my God.

"I am sooooo sorry," I say.

"Maeve," my co-leader speaks my magical name, "The Goddess does not apologize for her existence."

The group laughs, and so do I.

WHAT HAPPENS WHEN THE GODDESS APOLOGIZES: A SHORT CASE STUDY

I had a certain client a few years ago. Smart – she was an Ivy League–educated lawyer. Capable – her jam was creating content-rich websites that attracted visitors and sold them an evergreen program. Her first three sites were serving the Latino community. They were also making some $10k or so on autopilot. From entirely organic traffic.

She was looking to quit her law firm job and go full-time, which was why she was working with me. She wanted to offer her website creation services to others who wanted a turnkey, profit-on-autopilot income stream.

Of course, it was scary. She couldn't do it all herself – she needed an agency. First, though, we needed the offer.

The problem was, she couldn't get over the inner game. She couldn't get over the inner shame. Shame of being awesome? Shame of getting everything she ever wanted?

I had no idea. Except I did know that she was in some major shame because she could not stop apologizing.

"Elizabeth, I'm late today, I'm so sorry."

"Elizabeth, my payment is late, I'm so sorry."

"I know, I know, I was supposed to do my homework – I'm so sorry."

Even simple coaching and suggestions resulted in apologies – apologies for all the reasons why she didn't have her goal yet, all the reasons why she had not met her own standards of success yet.

"Oh, I know I should have picked an ideal client by now – I am so *sorry!*"

What is up with this Goddess? I thought. *Why is she apologizing for what she hired me to help her with?*

I might be forgetting a few details, here. I did not, however, forget my internal reaction.

What was most striking, most uncomfortable, was how all that apologizing made *me* feel. It was visceral. I found myself twisting, shrinking, contracting right along with her. It felt like I'd been slimed on, a heavy mantle of sticky that I couldn't wrestle my way out of, and the more I struggled the tighter and heavier that blanket became.

Hang on a second, I thought, somewhere in the middle of the third or fourth session of this.

Is that... shame?

I was brought back to that Equinox many years previous.

Wow.

This is what happens when the Goddess apologizes for her existence.

So, what's the problem with apologizing for your existence (hint: it's all pretty much apologizing for your existence)?

Let's be real, in addition to marveling at the spectacle of the Goddess apologizing for her existence, I was grossed out in no small part because, the whole thing felt very familiar.

I mean, it's not like I've never apologized like that. (Oh, wait – who, me?)

Which made that moment the Greatest Pattern Interrupt on the Planet.

Because what the *actual what*?

This person – my client – was and is a total rock star.

If you're reading this book, you are a rock star.

High-performing, ambitious women – we're all a bunch of freaking rock stars.

So, what are we doing with all of this apologizing?

Of course, we know the answer to that. As women, we've been conditioned to dim our light, hide, apologize for our existence. There's the patriarchal programming, and then on top of that, we have the cultural programming of lack, and on top of *that*, all of the childhood wounds that have grown into patterns and programming.

What's important for us to realize now, here, in this moment, in the light of day, is just how fricking incongruent and messed up all of that apologizing is.

I mean, what the hell are we apologizing for?

What on earth could we have possibly done that was so wrong??

Sure, I bumped a table at an inopportune moment all those years ago. My client was too busy to do her homework. Does that merit all the carrying on? Does it merit all of the deep shame we feel underneath?

No, it does not. Which is why I say, it's *all* apologizing for our existence.

I mean, why *else* would high-performing women

be carrying on in this way when there is nothing to apologize for.

Also? Just for fun because we're here? The energy of misdirected, misapplied, shame-filled apology, from someone who has zero business apologizing is downright gross.

Which is why, dear Goddess, your excessive apologizing has got to go.

By the way, just in case it wasn't clear, there's a lot more to the apologizing game we play (more on the specifics of the game in a second) than simply saying, "Oops, sorry."

Here are a few apologies you might be making that you might not even know you're making:

(Of course, take what resonates with you and leave the rest. My point isn't to make an exhaustive list; it's to uncover hidden apologies that have to go.)

Every time you write a post and then don't post it – or, better yet, post it and then delete it – because you're secretly afraid that it was too much, you might be apologizing.

Every time you want to tell a client a hard truth and then back down, you might be apologizing.

Every time you want to show up strong but then back off because, "What will people think?" you might be apologizing.

Every time you dim your light to make someone else feel more comfortable …

Every time something you say or do makes

someone uncomfortable, and then you feel bad, guilty, wrong, or ashamed …

All of these are apologies.

Now, are there legit times for saying you're sorry? Of course.

But the simple fact is, for so many strong, powerful women, those times really truly are few and far between.

Because we take on so much that isn't ours, make others' feelings more important than our own, take responsibility for hurts and slights and bad feelings in others when who knows what's actually going on with them – and is it even our problem *anyway* (hint: probably not) – apologizing becomes a habit. And the effects of apologizing become internalized. The habit of apologizing reflects our deep shame (which isn't even ours), which leads us to unconsciously believe that we have something to apologize for (we don't), which leads to – you guessed it – more apologizing (and around and around we go).

And the worst of it?

We're shooting ourselves in the foot with this, digging ourselves an even deeper hole, because insecurity is a huge turn-off. The shame is so palpable, even when stifled, it makes people wildly uncomfortable.

Especially ultra-premium clients – those best-of-the-best clients for your most expensive, deep-dive programs.

The truth is… clients (and team) don't want to feel all of that shame. They have enough of their own, they don't need yours, or anyone else's, on top of it.

Thou art Goddess, and so is everybody else. The Goddess does not apologize for her existence. As a Divine Be-ing (just like everybody else), you get to take up the space befitting of your Divine Nature.

THE DIVINE TRUTH (AND DEEPER INCONGRUENCE)

So we know that thou art Goddess, and so is everybody else.

You are Divine. You are a Creator Being.

For all of the reasons previously listed, apologizing for our existence does not make sense.

We can't hold the energy of being divine or being multidimensional or the energy for epic expansion and hold the space of apology for our own existence at the same time.

Those two things are completely incongruent.

One is Truth; the other is flat-out untrue.

And make no mistake, when you apologize for your existence, you apologize for, well, being *you*.

When you are at your Highest Level, when you are embodying your *divine* self …

You *embrace* your greatness.

You *embrace* your gifts, talents, and skills.

You *embrace* your expertise.

You *embrace* your amazing judgment.

You *embrace* your "faults."

You *embrace* your humanity.

You *embrace* your *Desire*. You *claim* what you want.

You *embrace* your expansive nature.

I could go on. My point is you *embrace* these things rather than apologize for them.

And you *embrace* your fees and what is *required* – of you and of others.

Now I think you can see that "no apologies" does not mean that you never apologize.

Taking 100 percent responsibility (full ownership) of our results is absolutely required if we want to create what we want. In our programs and with our clients, we take ownership of a screw-up and make things right.

But ask yourself, how *often* is that kind of apology – where you did something "bad," and you feel you "need" to apologize – how often is that *really* required?

Not very often.

WHERE THE NEED TO APOLOGIZE *REALLY* COMES FROM

There are some very interesting tools that humans wield against themselves.

There's the threat of not belonging to or being kicked out of the tribe. (This is our greatest and most primal fear.) There's the threat of not being seen or being misunderstood.

And perhaps the most insidious of all... there's shame.

What's interesting is that the first two are used by others. The third, shame, is one that is used by others to get us to turn against ourselves.

Then, we form the habit of turning it against ourselves... and we keep using it.

For example, we do something that someone doesn't like. Maybe we offend our mother or something when we're young. We are too loud in the grocery store or the car, maybe.

Our mother says something that is meant to cause shame. Now, we could let it go, but chances are good that because we want to belong and because we trust our mother and want to be loved and she is our hero, instead we feel a little bit of shame.

Then, later, we're too loud on the school bus. We're too much in class. We do something "wrong."

We already know what to do. We pick up the shame knife and use it against ourselves. And we do it without thinking.

Later, an even more insidious use of shame can take hold: shame as bypass. You did something wrong, so you have to feel bad about it. And because you're hurting, it's okay to keep your Desires at arm's length. Indeed, keeping your Desires at arm's length is another form of punishment.

Years ago, one of my mentors had a phrase for this truth. "Guilt and shame are the most effective forms of disempowerment."

And they are. From a dark persuasion, dark magic perspective, they are among the most effective ways to manipulate someone else. Because we turn the shame knife against ourselves!

And we never stop to think about it. We never stop to question what or whose standards we might not be meeting. Indeed, we carry the habit from other generations. So we completely miss the fact that the trifecta of guilt-shame-apology does *not* come from you. (Though you use them against yourself.)

The guilt-shame-apology trifecta comes from *not* meeting others' standards for you, or somehow what you do falls into what others think of as "bad and wrong."

When you apologize for your gifts, being big, and so on, you're butting up against someone else's ideas and standards. You're butting up against group consciousness. You apologize and dim your light, but that shame is not yours to carry.

It's time to bust out of that entire cycle. It's time for a new standard.

The No Apologies Standard is where we break the habit of apologizing for existing and instead take radical responsibility: for our actions, Desires, and creating what we want.

When we activate the No Apologies Standard, we

activate self-love and acceptance. We activate love and acceptance of others (because we don't expect them to apologize, either).

The No Apologies Standard could also be the self-love standard. You love and accept yourself fully – no matter what you did, or what is going on.

You take ownership and make it right.

IT'S ALL ABOUT ME

Have you noticed a little something else that happens, when you are in the energy of apology?

Your brain conveniently ignores …

- All of your years of experience
- The hundreds if not thousands of clients you have helped
- All of the clients who have been through your program and have been successful
- All of the clients who have been to the program and have paid in full

And so many other forms and expressions of your personal power.

Of course, a great deal of what we experience as shame is informed by wounds and traumas. We really need to name that.

However, there is more.

If we approach shame and apology from the space

of *be*-ing in the space of the Divine *Be*-ing (what we call "Magician Brain" – where you step out of 3D perspective and into that of your Highest Level), we can notice that this ignoring is, paradoxically, very ego-based and me-focused.

Let's *not* make this bad or wrong, of course. Oh, the irony!

However, as a transformational leader who is truly stepping into the space of be-ing with and embodying your Divine Nature, and Divine Energy in general – your divinity and divine frequency – we get to notice if that's what we *really* want to do.

PRACTICAL APPLICATION: CALLING IN YOUR NEXT LEVEL OR HIGHEST LEVEL CLIENTS

So there you are – a Leader having done all of the work. And yet, you're still rocking the energy of apology. And its annoying little cousin: asking for permission.

Can I really go for these clients?

Can I offer this program?

Is it okay to charge this much?

Oh, I'm so sad that that's too much money for you; here, let me discount it.

Oh, I'm so sorry that you're unhappy; what can I do to make it right?

(Note: In transformational leadership, the customer is *not* always right.)

And then there's the more subtle forms:

Oh, I didn't do enough for you.

Oh, you didn't get the results.

You didn't get the results that, apparently, I promised.

Oh, it must be my fault.

Oh, it's all on me.

This is what Leaders can do! And yet this is what I know for sure after soooo many years teaching so many Leaders to attract clients, fill their programs, and grow their businesses:

Ultra-premium clients, and your Highest Level of clients, do *not* want you to apologize. At all.

Why? To get back to the confidence thing, they are *paying* you for something else.

They are *paying* you to show up whole and complete. They are paying you to love yourself.

(Yes, self-love is a practice when you're accepting money to help others transform!)

My clients would not get such amazing results if I was apologizing all the time, and you would not be having the same experience reading this book if I was apologizing all the time.

So if clients don't want apology, what *do* they want?

They want confidence. They want expectation. They want your Divine Nature.

They want you to be who you really are – *without* apology.

ZERO F**KS GIVEN

Can you remember the last time you just said "f**k it" and did what was true to you anyway? Despite whom you might piss off or what others might think?

Felt good, didn't it? Well guess what: *you can feel that way all the time!*

And really, that's what the No Apologies Standard invites us to step into.

It's not that we don't care or never apologize.

But we've let go of the sticky shame. We've let go of the weapons installed by others for use against ourselves.

Your clients want the same. And when you model it for them, they see it, get it, and break the shame spirals of their own.

To complete this chapter, I'll give you a simple inquiry.

Where are you holding back or secretly apologizing?

Wherever it is, I invite you to let that go.

Own who you are. Take up space.

No Apologies is full self-expression in action.

That, my friend, is very magnetic.

10

THE BENEVOLENT QUEEN
STANDARD

I t was a "hair on fire" moment when I got the resignation letter.

We had *just* enrolled fifteen people into an eight-week, high-touch, high-ticket program. The program was about to begin.

I was already feeling strapped. I was still the only one delivering the service in our programs – that is, the only one helping our clients get the *results* – and this was (and still is) a "high service" sort of engagement. Our magic – helping clients create offers that are so spot on that they sell without sales calls – is a hands-on, iterative process. And I was already the one who would be doing all of the iterating.

So, our business manager was crucial to the operation. In addition to pushing the train on all the usual admin stuff (call times, community, "where's the recording?") and leading our "doers" to a high level of delivery, she would also be the one who held firm when clients tried to back out of their commitment, when things got hard, the fear kicked in, and they started wiggling and making excuses.

Which – I knew from experience – it *would*. Packaging up your magic is a transformational process, after all.

So… receiving the resignation letter, at the most inopportune time, was also an "Oh, shit."

Now, let's be real. The truth is, we always know. It wasn't a huge surprise that our business manager chose to resign, nor was it a huge surprise that she chose to do it when I was in a vulnerable spot. This is one of the human ways that humans be humaning – picking the most inopportune time for things.

I thought I had more time.

Nope. Turns out, I did *not* have more time.

First things first: try to stay calm. Next: triage. Call the nurse, who could help me stop the bleeding, and – more importantly – get my bearings. That turned out to be who it always is in these weird "team" moments: my longtime colleague and respected acquaintance Tina Forsyth, creator of the OBM (Online Business Manager) industry.

"Aaaaaaahhhh!" I said.

"Breathe," said Tina. "You see what an opportunity you have here, right?"

It took some doing, but within an hour, I could see the *real* crossroads I was at. The real "Hecate moment," so to speak. (Hecate, goddess of the cross-roads, crone, initiator, shatteror of *all* illusions.)

The opportunity was far more than I thought it would be. In short, it was this:

In that moment, I had the opportunity to slap on the Band-Aid. To hire another "online business manager" – someone who would come in, keep her arms around all the things (as the last business manager had been doing – no small part of which was responsible for the burnout which led to her leaving), and keep us dogpaddling along.

Or …

I could step into a different space. I could show up as the CEO, the magician at the top of the mountain, wielding her wand for a very different outcome than "getting by" or even "make $300k plus my salary per year."

I could be thrown by the circumstances, or I could use the circumstances as an opportunity to say, "*This* is how it's going to be."

I could show up as the Benevolent Queen.

I did not spend the past dozen years honing my craft in all the areas to just dog paddle. I'm building something significant. I'm building something that is destined to be much bigger. And damnitall…

It is done, it is done, it is done.

This is how it is, and that's how it is.

The Benevolent Queen had arrived.

WHO IS THE BENEVOLENT QUEEN?

The Benevolent Queen is the part of you who is the ruler of your life and business.

She gives the commands. Hires and fires. Makes those high-level decisions. Runs the show.

Like a queen, she rules over her loyal subjects. Who are her loyal subjects? Your resources. Things like money, time, energy, attention, and yes, your relationships.

As a queen, the Benevolent Queen is a ruler. She is a leader. Unlike some actual monarchs, though, she is never a dictator. She is the benevolent queen. Therefore, she rules with love, kindness, and respect. She understands that her loyal subjects contribute to her and contribute to the whole system. She sees her "subjects" for the contributions that they are.

But make no mistake... the Benevolent Queen is queen. She makes the hard decisions. She faces the music, as I did with the business manager situation. She has the final say and what she says, goes. And her loyal subjects act accordingly.

If the Benevolent Queen oversteps her bounds, or her subjects don't agree with how they're being led, they have the power to leave. They can leave any time. Whether they stay or go is entirely dependent, of course, on how the Benevolent Queen shows up.

Because the Benevolent Queen is benevolent, she wants to partner with her subjects. She wants to keep them happy. She wants them to feel loved and cared for. She wants full buy-in and acts accordingly.

So, her subjects co-create and cooperate. They know their role: to support the queen.

The Benevolent Queen's energy is grounded, centered, anchored in her co-creative power. She knows that what she says, goes. Because she is the queen.

The Benevolent Queen understands magic. She understands that that which she says is done, that which she truly chooses, is done on the non-physical plane. It is already done.

Her motto is: "This is how it is, and that's how it is."

THE BENEVOLENT QUEEN'S INVITATION: TO ACCEPT YOUR POWER TO CO-CREATE

The Benevolent Queen lives inside all of us. (If you're a man, you can change this energy to the Benevolent King, if it suits you. Or not.)

The Benevolent Queen represents our greatest power: our power to choose.

When we step into the Benevolent Queen, we accept a higher level of choosing. We give up all remaining illusions of victimhood. We acknowledge that we may have been a victim, and we honor that experience, rather than denying it. And we also acknowledge that we have extraordinary co-creative power. We choose to anchor in on the power side of the line, which is an internal shift first.

We accept a higher level of personal responsibility. We accept all responsibility, which is our power to create.

When we step into the Benevolent Queen, we go from "this just is" to making it *real* in our life. This is how it is, and that's how it is. For you.

As you might imagine, the Benevolent Queen is a radical departure from the status quo. Most people, through no "fault" of their own, are woefully unaware of the creative power they carry, the power that is naturally a part of them. When and if they do learn of it, very few people fully accept it.

All of this is A-OK. The Benevolent Queen is not about judgment. Indeed, as we'll see, one main part of the Benevolent Queen's job is to right the scales, tip the balance from victimhood to personal power, remove or eliminate the dynamic of "power over vs. power under" – even when "ruling," even as a Queen.

The Benevolent Queen is a model of power at its purest and most beneficial. She is a model of what's possible.

We are conditioned, and constantly told through imprinting, programming, and so on that we don't have any power.

And let's be real... we don't have *all* the power. There *are* things that are outside of our control. There *are* very real people and forces in power who are *not* benevolent, who make the destructive power grabs, who have *no* regard for human life, who want to perpetuate the illusions of "no power" so they can keep all the power for themselves.

The Benevolent Queen recognizes our greatest personal power, which is our power to choose. She makes careful, intentional, clear choices. She co-creates.

Through the Benevolent Queen, you will take your power back and put it where it belongs: with you.

A TYPICAL POWER LEAK (IN THE LIFE OF A LEADER)

Let's say you're in the middle of a launch. It's a bigger launch. You took several months to write all the content, you hired a launch manager to make sure that it goes off without a hitch, and you have several of your colleagues with big lists promoting it. You were ultra- high-energy in the marketing leading up to the big reveal. You gave the webinar to end all webinars. And then...

Crickets.

You start to panic. Racing thoughts. *OMG this is tanking. Why the hell aren't they signing up? Can't they see that this is perfect for them? What are you going to do?*

Hold it right there.

It's easy to think in a situation like this that you

are a victim to circumstance. And, I mean, let's be honest – when a launch is tanking, how easy is it to flip the attention and the reason why to your people? (*They're* not the right people. *They're* not signing up, etc.)

Without getting too caught up in the mechanics of launching, the Truth is that all of that line of thinking (that it's them and they) is an illusion. It's also an illusion that you have no way out of it and that your business is going to be forever doomed.

The feeling like your broken launch will never get back on track is *also* an illusion.

And yet – the brain, Brian – sees these illusions as Truth, tells us they're Truth, and so you run around acting as if they are Truth.

They're not Truth.

So the Benevolent Queen, who knows the truth, and knows that she is here to guide and lead her loyal subject, Brian, because lord knows he can't do it all on his own, says:

The Truth is my clients are always there. The Truth is the money is already here. The Truth is there are a zillion possibilities. If this launch doesn't work – and it might not, we might not be able to get it back on track – then there is another way that will. Marketing Truth and psychology of human beings tells me pretty clearly that I didn't quite hit it with my offering. Because if my offering was hitting the real pain points, and if my messaging was really talking to the right people, some of them would be buying.

I choose to allow in $100,000 in the next two weeks. I choose to do the very best that I can with this launch. I choose to find out what my clients really want. I choose higher ground. This is how it is, and that's how it is.

Turning circumstances into Truth is how we give our power away.

The Benevolent Queen knows Truth and returns the power to where it belongs.

BEING IN RIGHT RELATIONSHIP WITH YOUR POWER

The deeper magic of the Benevolent Queen, and how we activate her in our life, lies in understanding how she changes our relationship to power and how we use our power in relation to others.

For many, many years – probably all the years that "personal growth" has been around – the transformation industry has had a skewed view of power, a misidentified and misapplied approach to power, and, as such, has perpetuated harmful "power practices" that are crying to be shifted.

The biggest one of these is the "power over / power under" dynamic: I am the leader, I am the authority (or "auth-or-i-tah," for all my South Park friends), you will do as I say. I've created "the success"; you want that success for yourself. I have the system; therefore, what I say is really important, and you should listen to me and do as I do.

"Power over / power under" is a group consciousness dynamic. It has fear at the root, so it has to perpetuate itself with more fear.

And allll of the marketing and sales strategies then back this up. Live events – seminars – are structured for maximum persuasion and sales. Emails engage the amygdala and press the fear and envy buttons, leading to "I must buy this, or I will not survive!" The rules of marketing are used to sell the most, the most often.

Pretty messed up for an industry that purports to empower people, isn't it?

Power is a tricky dance. On the light side of the equation, the fact is Resistance is a Thing. Brian and what he does with our brains is *real*.

Years ago, one of my copywriting teachers used to say, "Elizabeth, your real 'competition' is never your competitor's product. It's your clients' own inertia. It is a mini miracle when they actually pull out their credit card and buy from you, because of allll that they had to overcome internally to do it. Respect that."

So on the one hand, persuasion is a good thing. The fact is, as transformational leaders, we are enrolling from the first minute that our potential client encounters us, and every moment thereafter. It is required to even be able to bring our people to the point of empowered decision.

Ah, but yes – empowered decision is what we

want. Not, "You must follow me, or you will lose love." Or, "You must buy my product, or you will lose security."

Earlier I shared the beautiful metaphor we use at 7-Figure Goddess® for the energy that we want to command at our marketing. *Would you like to sit at our table?*

If you're a vegan, it's a vegan smorgasbord. If you're low-carb, like I am, it's all the delectable, low-carb veggies and nourishing food that will never spike blood sugar – and yummy desserts that have been made over to satisfy the craving without doing the same.

We want clients to see our table and see that we have what they already want. We do a lot of picture painting, to fill in the picture of that table. And, yes, to help them see the blind spots they have – because there are a lot of them.

Then we can say, "Oh, hey, do you want to sit at our table?"

And they can *choose* to sit down… or not.

The Benevolent Queen operates in a similar manner. She understands her power. She knows she has power, and she knows that she is setting a pretty damned awesome table for her subjects, by respecting and honoring them and giving them what they want. (And yes: resources like time and money are energies that respond to energies – i.e., ways of *be*-ing, just as people do.)

So, there's no need to coerce or force. What's more, she knows she's the queen, so she knows that she doesn't have to flaunt her queen-ness before her subjects.

She also knows that she needs them, just as much as they need her. Therefore, they have power, too.

So, ultimately, rather than pushing or forcing, the Benevolent Queen knows that she will get a lot further with respect for others' power rather than forcing using her own. While at the same time – knowing, full well, that the buck stops with her.

She is "large and in charge." To wield that, in a way that creates more life for all, she must use her power in a way that meets others' power.

This is the energy of Divine Equanimity – Divine to Divine, peer to peer, both acknowledging the power structure, each honoring the other.

This is the dynamic. The question is, after being in a place where we do not recognize this, where we have felt until now that we either have to submit or dominate,

How do we step into this fully? How do we activate the energy of the Benevolent Queen?

THE TRUTH THAT FLIES IN THE FACE OF HISTORY AND CIRCUMSTANCE

So what does this look like in *practice*? What does it mean to *live* this standard?

The first way to live this standard is the bigger awareness that nothing and nobody has power over you, other than the power you give to people and things.

Yes, we live in a world where oppression still exists. "Power over" is a very real experience.

And, at the same time, you are a Divine Be-ing. You are the same substance as God. You are from God, you are of God.

You have the same power that She has because we are one and the same substance.

You have the same creative power as God and Goddess. (Remember, so does everybody else.)

With that awareness, the invitation before you is to come to believe, and know, in your very bones, that *nothing* has power over you.

You are the master of everything in your life.

Nothing has power over you. You have power over your life.

This does not mean circumstances don't happen. Of course, they do.

It also doesn't mean that people in power never take our right to choose. Of course, they do.

Ah, but we have that power to choose. And understanding that awareness – really, really getting it – returns that power to you. Even when you are dealing with circumstances that may say otherwise.

It means that creative domain lies *within you*, no matter what. Always. Always.

Our greatest power is our power to choose. About everything.

This means consciously letting go of the idea that *circumstance* runs the show, that circumstance somehow has power over you, and coming into the true understanding that the Field, Creative Life Force Energy, is, at its core, neutral and that as such, it can be directed, and that it will give us right back the same energy that we put into it. Love is met with love. Fear is met with fear.

PRACTICAL APPLICATION: MONEY RESPONDS TO YOUR ENERGY

Our favorite practical application of the Benevolent Queen is money.

Have you ever felt like money had power over you? Like money was in control, not you?

Maybe not consciously. But if we look at how the collective consciousness conditions us around money (money doesn't grow on trees, rich people are bad, there's never enough, etc.), we see a lot of issues of power.

Money is energy; money is a resource, which means that money has a power attached to it. People in power have used that in many ways throughout history to control the collective.

You may or may not relate to the idea of money

having power over you. You may say, "Yeah, I've had that" or "No way have I had that."

However, I'll invite you to notice that you've given your power away with money if:

You've said no to something you truly desired in your heart because of money.

You've had an argument with someone you love over money and felt victimized.

You've ever felt shame around money – remember, shame is an exceptional tool for disempowerment.

You've ever contracted your energy or hidden parts of yourself because of money.

You've ever hidden something regarding money or money behaviors.

You've ever felt powerless to attract the money you want, when you want it.

You've ever tried to "get money."

You've told yourself you can't afford it.

You've ever felt like you had to do something or could not do something because of money.

In all of these scenarios, money has had the power, not you. You've chosen to buy into the illusion that money runs the show.

You've made money your master.

Again, this is a very group consciousness thing to do. Also, "power over" with money is a very real thing. Here, though, we want to bring awareness to Truth.

So, we can activate this Standard in a very practical way by righting the power relationship with money. By giving back the power we've given it over us and instead invite it to co-create with us.

This means consciously letting go of the idea that money runs the show, that money somehow has power over you, coming into understanding of money's true nature as neutral energy that can be aligned with and directed and accepting responsibility for money's presence in your life or not.

See, what distinguishes – not separates but distinguishes us from everything else is our power to choose. Money doesn't have a power to choose. It's just an energy and responds to us. Money isn't sentient; we are. So we don't want to give money power by putting it over or under us.

Come into right relationship and direct the energy. This is the first way to activate the Benevolent Queen. (And money is *such* a great place to do it, because we get immediate gratifying feedback when the relationship shifts.)

Become aware of money's true nature – which is energy. Consciousness. Just like you, money is made of creative substance. It is neutral energy that will *respond* to you, just like creative substance will.

Reaffirm your acceptance of full responsibility for money's presence in your life.

"Money will come when you call it." This is one of my favorite quotes from Bob Proctor.

How do you call it? By holding standards around

money. Starting with the standard of not giving it power. And then of course by energetic attraction followed by aligned action.

If we want money, we have to stop making it all powerful and wake up to the fact that we create it and call it in – or not – based on our own decision and direction.

Finally, with this standard comes a next- level embodiment and understanding of where the money comes from.

Do not confuse be-ing Goddess with being the source of your income.

You are not the Source of your income. Source, she who I call Goddess, is the Source of your income.

You are the contribution, the channel, the catalyst – not the Source.

When you are playing the "I am the Source" game, then all the money has to come from your 3D energy and your 3D actions.

When you are the Contribution, you are Divine Energy and the channel through which divine energy can flow. You have infinite resources, infinite energy, infinite access to abundance.

So cool, right?

This is just a matter of being hyper-aware of this truth and reminding yourself that it is, in fact, true. And some pattern-busting, because most of us have quite a bit of this going on.

THE TRUTH TO HOLD OUT IN FRONT OF YOU

If you're a comics fan, or even if you're not and you've just watched all the Marvel movies of the past ten years (or maybe one or two of them), you've heard of Spider-Man's famous awareness , the lesson taught by Uncle Ben before the worst happens.

"With great power, comes great responsibility."

As you may have noticed by now, all of the Standards get back to the Divine Standard.

Thou art Goddess. (And so is everybody else.)

You are a Divine Be-ing, which comes with great power.

With that great power comes great responsibility, too. First and foremost is the responsibility of accepting that power, along with the acceptance of everyone else's power, and being the Queen of your Life, "ruling" not by force but by Divine Equanimity, conscious co-creation, and creativity.

The Benevolent Queen Standard will change you. It will instantly give you access to more of your power, more of the time.

And it will change those around you. Because as you be the Divine Be-ing you be, you will wake others up. And show them the expansive, loving, more-life-to-all way that this thing called "power" can be done.

11

THE MONEY IMPECCABILITY STANDARD

I couldn't believe what I was hearing.

"I'm sorry , this program just isn't in alignment for me. It's not working. The people in it just aren't my people. Last month was my last payment. I'm out."

It was 2015. The program in question was a relatively small mastermind – twelve people. The client in question had found me right before the doors closed.

So we didn't know each other all that well when she joined, but when she signed up, she threw herself into it, headfirst. She even flew all the way to California from Australia to participate in our first retreat. She had also written me several emails raving about my content and how our program was "the way" and was completely saving her business.

Now, though, she was telling me that she wanted out.

I'd been in business for seven years at that point. So, it certainly wasn't the first "back out" conversation I'd ever had to have.

Nonetheless, I was furious. *How dare she!* She signed a contract saying she would honor all her payments. To back out was a breach of contract and not in integrity.

How can one purport to be a transformational leader – and want to ask for those big fees – and then, on the other hand, turn around and break commitments to other practitioners who pour time, energy attention, and money into providing the services that the backer-outer *voluntarily* signed up for?

As I read "the email" this time around, I was annoyed. And, to be honest, fearful. Because I knew what was about to unfold.

Sure enough, one by one, I received "the email" from one, then two, then three, then four more people who had been a part of the group.

"Sorry, I have to leave."

"I'm not going to be able to pay you this month."

"It's not you, it's me. Sorry."

"Please don't charge my card again."

I let the triggers come and let the anger wash over me. Then I had to sit with more discomfort. I knew why this was happening. I knew what of my own behavior had contributed to it. Not caused it. Because clients always have a role in these exchanges. If you are as open and honest about the program as possible, then they know what they are getting into as they sign their contracts.

Energy, however, follows energy. As Leader, I knew that my energy was setting the stage and that allowing one person to back out (without turning them over to legal) would trigger a whole host of money messes and further backing out.

The truth was, I wasn't in integrity, either.

After licking my wounds a little, I rolled up my sleeves and dove into emails and conversations.

It was time for a new standard.

YOUR LINE IN THE SAND: THE MONEY IMPECCABILITY STANDARD

The Money Impeccability Standard is an interesting one. In a way, it's very cut and dry. There's not a lot of ambiguity and not a lot of complicated esoteric shizz to understand here. So let's get right to it.

It might sound harsh. It might sound judge-y. (If it does, I invite you to just notice rather than react.) It might sound a little "separation consciousness."

It is none of those things. Indeed, done with commitment and love and from a place of the Divine Standard ("thou art Goddess, and so is everybody else"), the Money Impeccability Standard may very well be the most freeing and the most healing Standard of all.

The Money Impeccability Standard is the zero tolerance policy for money drama of any kind – from *anybody*, and that includes you.

This means:

- No late payments
- No missed payments
- No invoices that are hanging out there for thirty days waiting to be paid
- No allowing people to stay in your programs when they owe you money
- No endless listening to people's money drama stories
- No emails to clients that take you forty-five minutes or more to write.
- No ninety-minute conversations with people who have no intention of paying you.
- No allowing your business to *bleed* money
- No *years* spent in the "money fog" where you haven't a flippin' clue about where your money is going
- No making it okay for people to bring money drama into your space (this includes your team)
- No allowing *money drama* to run the show.

Being in business for yourself, and then growing bigger, means looking money in the eyes. It also means that money drama is going to show up sooner or later: clients who bring the drama, vendors who bring the drama... maybe even you're the one bringing the drama!

Your business is going to push your money buttons. Money Impeccability means becoming lovingly fierce about eliminating any kind of money drama from your life and energy field.

And I do mean lovingly fierce.

Money, as we know, is, like everything, an energy of the Divine. And it's a very 3D thing. It's a playing field where all our 3D behaviors, patterns and opportunities for growth get played out. It's at the base of the pyramid, the root of our 3D security, the foundation of just about every decision we make.

But money is Creative Life Force Energy. Money is the same energy as God is the same energy as *you*.

The money that you accept from clients is *their* energy. That's a very precious thing indeed.

It's the energy of *more life*.

As those who are a commitment to walking in the world at our Highest Level – we also get to be a stand for the Truth of money.

The Truth of money as energy and a very pure energy form – *not* all that stuff we've projected onto it.

We get to accept, even embrace, release, and

return to Source all of these patterns within us and model what that looks like.

This is the Money Impeccability Standard. It will set you free.

THE TRUTH ABOUT MONEY DRAMA AND WHY IT HAS TO GO

On the surface, things like getting "the email" are annoying. Juggling money around between accounts is annoying. It can push all of the shame buttons (there's that shame thing again) and have us go, "I thought I handled this already?"

It can make you feel really, really bad. It's quite interesting, isn't it? How we can be fully rocking the Confidence Standard one minute, but then it takes a scold-y email from a credit card company ("Your payment is due!") to knock us off our high and have Brian come running. *See! I told you you were a complete f**k-up when it comes to money! It's what you are and it's what you always and forever will be!*

This shizz is hard. How hard it is should be reason enough to really get the money thing together and "heal the money wound" already. (As if it were that easy.)

Unfortunately, as you head into "collapse time to seven figures" land... as you want your business to become bigger than you, there is an even more compelling reason to clean up the money drama, draw a line in the sand, and simply, fiercely, lovingly show it the door and not allow it to come back in.

And that reason is *risk*.

Believe it or not, as your business grows bigger, a big part of your job, as leader of your business or CEO, is to manage risk: to look for problems, see what can go wrong, spot them in advance, and fix them.

Yes, I know this isn't exactly sexy. Them's the facts, though. Once things in your business are firing on all cylinders – things are humming, clients are signing up, the team is rocking – your main objective as CEO is expansion. A big part of that is ensuring that things don't break along the way!

Money drama causes "money breaks." It puts your business at risk. If you have employees, they need the cash flow from your business to live on. If you can't pay the credit card company, that's a problem.

As CEO, the buck stops with you. This is a lot of inner pressure. Many people don't want to feel the pressure, so they avoid it. They never "go there." You, on the other hand, have made the decision to go there. You're going there. So, notice that pressure and notice how it causes Inner Friction. The thoughts that make everything feel hard.

You can't operate at your Highest Level and perpetually operate with a lot of money risk.

That's not to say that you never take any money

risk – indeed, big money risks are the stuff from which big growth is made!

But if we don't have the foundation of impeccable money behavior, we create more friction, more pressure, more drama. Ultimately, all of these things waste a ton of time.

Loosey-goosey money boundaries puts your business at risk. This has been one of the huge motivators for me personally. I have a family and people who depend on my company. I have a mission. Life on earth in each incarnation is short, and we go through this forgetting before the next incarnation. There comes a point where you just do not mess around.

A SHORT LIST OF MONEY DRAMA

Here are just SOME of potential areas of money drama that you might be allowing, right now.

Note that not every situation here is "drama" for every person, as ultimately, what passes for money drama will be different for every person. Nonetheless, I invite you to use these as starting points to create a list of your own.

1. Client payments – payments must be made in full (if you have payment plans, the specific installment payment must be paid in full) and on time. No exceptions.

2. Vendor payments you owe – payments must be made in full and on time.

3. Feast or famine – allowing your business to run on fumes instead of commanding that the business take care of its own financial needs.

4. Excessive debt – taking on debt that you don't really need and then tolerating money stress.

5. Team that doesn't deliver – improperly training your team, not training your team, expecting your team to lead themselves instead of providing leadership to be at their best.

6. Back taxes, paperwork you need to file, etc.

7. Money avoidance – not having a clear picture of where your money is going, not getting reports from your bookkeeper, not keeping good records.

8. Money hiding – such as concealing money activity from your spouse.

9. Key performance indicators – not having any indication of how well your team or products are performing.

10. Taking care of people / enabling others' poor money habits and decisions, such as kids who borrow from you!

11. Poor boundaries with clients – going over on time, spending tons of time outside of

sessions in emails / voice messages, allowing them to "bank" or not take their sessions (which then puts you in a position of "owing"), etc.

12. "Energetic open doors" with clients – client disappearing acts (clients who hire you but then never schedules sessions or schedule and then disappear), contracts that are on pause, etc. Set firm boundaries and release clients if necessary.

13. Service delivery leaks – not delivering what you promised or taking an inordinate amount of time to deliver what was promised.

14. Allowing service delivery leaks from others – not speaking up when vendors aren't making good on what they promised.

15. Low fees – taking on the responsibility for whether or not clients can pay (deciding in advance whether someone can pay or not, taking any "can they pay?" judgments into consideration without proper cause – i.e., *not* just your own ideas / perceptions). Fees need to reflect the value.

16. Not mastering the skill of clearly articulating value, including creating/building value in a sales conversation. "I don't know how to talk about my services / describe what I do."

17. Discounting or overstuffing your programs / packages (which is a form of discounting).

18. No written policies around money and how money is to be handled. These include things like declined payment policies, payment policies for new clients (how much do they need to pay and by when to secure their spot in your programs), and collections policies.

19. Tolerating team that doesn't follow / enforce your money policies.

20. Lack of contracts and legal agreements, for teams, vendors, and clients.

21. Lack of protection for your intellectual properly (from a place of stewardship, not scarcity or deficit).

IT STARTS WITH YOU: THE IMPORTANCE OF CONGRUENCE

Imagine, now, what it would be like if each of the dramas in *your* list was entirely cleaned up. They just didn't exist in your world anymore.

How good would you feel? How proud of yourself would you be? And, more importantly, how differently would you show up for your clients?

Money is a 3D thing. It's a physical plane tool. Part of the physical plane reality.

We, meanwhile, are 5D be-ings. We are Divine Beings. The more we lean into that awareness, and embody it, the more power to co-create that we have.

You may have heard of Maslow's Hierarchy of Needs?

At the bottom is physical security; at the top, self-actualization.

If we are truly embodying our potential as 5D beings, if that's where we want to be, then there is an incongruence to continuing to buy into the illusions that create money drama.

Handling our money stuff is required, not optional. Because…

Isn't it going to be a little bit *difficult* to tap into the entire stream of possibilities that is our Divine Nature if we're constantly worried about money, constantly in a place of "not enough," and constantly in a place of allowing money drama into our field?

If we want to walk the world as Divine Beings – if we are a stand for being a higher consciousness and bringing that to the planet, then we have to have the 3D shizzle handled.

Not perfect! Good heavens, no. But handled. Because it's the most obvious, and like it or not, we carry the collective perception that having money means we have a certain amount of power and choice,

Now, of course, we get to be gentle with ourselves along the way. Beating ourselves up (there's that shame again) for being "out of alignment," "being incongruent," or for allowing money drama is a setup for more disempowerment.

Coming into alignment / congruence takes time, bebe!

So, we hold Money Impeccability as a Standard.

We choose to be impeccable with our money and the energy in our field.

We back that up with action – which automatically brings us into alignment in the non-physical.

And then we make it real in form.

Money drama brings your frequency down. Money drama is one of the great frequency dimmers, let's say.

So, we get to be a stand for something *else*. We get to be a stand for the Highest Level Frequency with money. And that doesn't mean having a ton of money necessarily. But having impeccable standards with money.

On a practical level, money impeccability is important because to not be impeccable with money in your business or life means putting a lot of 3D friction in your path.

Money Drama equals lost money, lost time, lost impact, and a huge drain on your energy.

All of the things I posted here are huge time, energy, and money drains.

All of them create scarcity.

We can't elevate if we're still stuck in scarcity.

We can't serve if we're still stuck in scarcity.

From that place, let's take a deep breath and acknowledge that this is *hard*.

Money has been used to create separation and division. Money is tied to security and therefore perceived power.

I'm not saying that any of this is easy. And I'm not saying that you need to be perfect. And I'm going to really invite you to notice where you go into the shame spiral, here. Remember, shame is a blazingly effective tool of disempowerment.

What I am inviting you to take on is *impeccability* with money as the standard.

YOUR SECRET BELIEFS: THE INVISIBLE REASONS BEHIND MONEY DRAMA

This isn't meant to be a "money beliefs unpacking" or "money mindset" book.

Your beliefs that create your money reality are a big topic. The important thing, for this moment, now, is for you to become aware that, as always, it's your beliefs and things you tell yourself as true that create the money drama.

Your illusions create the money drama! So it's helpful to know what secret money beliefs are running the show.

While this is *not* a big "money beliefs unpacking" or "money mindset" book, there's actually a pretty simple way to uncover those secret beliefs that create the money drama. I'd like to share it with you now.

Ready?

Think of your *biggest* money mess. The *biggest* one you can think of!

Maybe it's getting out of $100k or more in debt. (Spoiler alert: I've done that, more than once.)

Maybe your house got foreclosed on.

Maybe it's just all the money drama in your business right *now*. Maybe, as you read this, you have five people all backing out at the same time, or payroll is due and you don't have money to pay it, or someone is stealing your intellectual property and then trying to make it look like you stole from them (yep, lived that one too!).

Whatever it is, call up the picture in your mind. Go ahead, I'll wait.

Make it big and bright. Then step into the picture.

Stay in there long enough to get the feel of it. (But don't stay so long that your energy tanks.)

Step out. Shake it off.

Now, ask yourself the "Money Beliefs Reveal" question:

What would someone have to believe in order to have *that* experience?

Whoosh. Sit with that for a sec. Write it down.

Now ask yourself again: "What else would someone have to believe in order to have *that* experience?"

And so on, until there are no more beliefs that you have access to.

Now, this one can be a doozy. It's important that you don't get sucked into the vortex. This is just collecting information.

Then ask yourself: How else is this running the money drama in my business? Find where some of those leaks are.

And then: What Truth will I operate by instead? And, What action will I take instead to start cleaning it up?

The key here is to stay neutral. Because your illusions are just illusions. They aren't who you are. Who *you* are is a Divine Be-ing. Thou Art Goddess, Goddess!

And here's the real kicker.

The more you start cleaning up the money drama – whether you really "believe" the new truth or not – the faster you will really, truly align with the new beliefs , the New Truth.

While we're here – let's talk about two beliefs that pretty much all of us have that contribute to money drama:

1. The belief that there's not enough (scarcity and lack – covered in the Abundance Standard chapter)

2. The belief that we're "bad" and / or have done something "wrong" and therefore must be punished (shame)

By now, you know the Truth. The Truth is Abundance. There is no lack, only lack-based circumstances. Your shame is not your own; rather, it is an internalized, conditioned response that is installed, consciously or unconsciously, by imperfect humans (who are passing on what they know or sometimes, acting maliciously) and collective programming that has been used to control humans for tens of thousands of years.

I invite you to see these for the illusion lies that they are from this moment forward.

And while you may continue to "work" on them as you go, remember that on the non-physical planes, transformation happens in an instant. It is done. The rest is allowing our very human forms to catch up.

You are a Divine Being having a physical experience, gifted with an intellect, powers of perception, the power to direct energy, and the power of choice.

PRACTICAL APPLICATION #1: LETTING PAYMENT DRAMA GO FOR GOOD

When it comes to holding Money Impeccability as a Standard in your business, to support your leap to seven figures in two years or less, there is no application that will have the most impact, in my experience, than that of payment arrangements: the allowing of money *in* and the honoring of sacred money commitments.

When a client steps into a program – any program – it requires commitment and agreement between client and transformational practitioner. There will be energy expended on both sides. In order for *you* to show up fully, you have to get paid.

Also, transformational leaders often miss the fact that, in order to call in those clients, there will be a cost. No client comes to you for free. Lead generation is one of the greatest expenses in your business.

On the client side, their money is an expression of *their* commitment. Stepping into a program is a big deal, so it can feel wobbly.

Your role, in that moment, is to hold firm to whatever money boundaries you've set up.

For example, a while back, I had a client who, after being given a full ten weeks to pay, was *still* late making payment on the date we had agreed on.

Had I just let it go without taking action, it would have changed the entire dynamic of our work together.

So I asked the team to set up a very strict payment policy to collect on what was owed. Also, she was not allowed to join any more programs.

Why do we allow money drama? A desire to be loving and caring, number one. We don't want to "hurt" anyone. Plus, Leaders have secret fears that they must put up with payment drama, or clients won't sign up.

Neither of these are true. We can't hurt anyone as a result of *their* choices.

And you absolutely *will* have clients. (Indeed, the stronger money boundaries you have, the more – and *more ideal* – clients you will have.)

When I was allowing for all that drama around being paid on time, that was a reflection of my own secret beliefs, of course. And they were really the illusions of scarcity – that I had to allow for this or I wouldn't have clients.

For someone else, it may be the illusion of unworthiness. I'm not worth it, I need to make it a struggle, I'm not allowed to have, etc.

Your invitation is to look at the patterns of money drama running in your business, and then peek under the hood. What are the deeper illusions that are running? And then you want to address them head on, within yourself. And within your team. Because in your business, all of this is going to show up with your team, too.

PRACTICAL APPLICATION #2: CLEAN UP ANY DRAMA

As we complete this chapter, here are four steps to hold the Money Impeccability Standard.

First, take an inventory. Where do you know you're allowing money drama or damaging money patterns into your life? Where are you falling into collective programming, ancestral programming, and illusion when it comes to money? Where are you out of alignment with the true nature of money?

The list given in this chapter will give you some ideas to start with.

Next, go through each and tune in, asking yourself what illusions or "negative beliefs" are running behind each one. Use the practice I shared.

Third, what is the Truth that you are going to hold out in front of you instead? What do you choose to live by?

Fourth, clean up the behavior.

What action do you know you need to take?

TRUTH: MONEY IS DIVINE ENERGY (MONEY IS DIVINE – JUST LIKE EVERYBODY ELSE!)

Money comes to you (both in business and outside) from Source, through other people. It is the energy of your clients' life minutes. It is the energy of their hopes and dreams.

When you are the steward of money in your business, you are leading your clients. Money Impeccability, and holding your clients to their commitments is part of what they are investing in. It creates value far greater than you know, even in the midst of discomfort. It leads to greater connection.

Back in 2015, when I got "the email" from the first client attempting to back out of my program, I got busy.

It was awkward. Clunky. I did some of the boundary-holding over email because it was just too uncomfortable. My team at the time couldn't hold the boundaries either. It was on me to step up.

Some of the clients did back out. They never paid me what they owed, and unfortunately, I had to release them from our community and take them to collections.

That first client who sent the first email chose a different path.

We set up a payment plan. She didn't want to stick with it, but she did. And she paid off the entire balance.

These days, she runs a seven-figure agency helping transformational leaders systematize and scale their businesses.

A few years after she completed her payment plan, she sent me a kind note, thanking me for holding her to a higher standard and requiring that she honor her agreements. She shared how it made her stronger as a leader and gave her permission to require that others honor *their* agreements.

Money Impeccability is transformation in action.

'

12

THE TRANSFORMATION
STANDARD

W hen it comes to our work, as transformational practitioners, is there anything better than messages like this from a client?

"Just reading the amazing advice you posted for me [in the group] last night…

"I want you and your team to know that after 3 other business coaches in three years since I decided to grow my business seriously, you're the only one who has actually helped me make the sales.

"And… so fast! Your systems, templates, and team are all extraordinary – you actually deliver what others promise.

"I'm so very grateful that you and the team held open the door for me to lead me through.

"I also want to mention your personal magic – you seem to carry a frequency around money that feels similar to my area of mastery.

It's not simply mastery, though… it's alchemical.
Thank you."

Not gonna downplay – it's messages like this that make it all worthwhile.

Maybe you can relate? After all, our egos need a little love as we work through all the pieces of business demanding our attention – the highs, the lows, the risks.

We all want our clients to get great results. This client, for example, has brought us tons of visibility and referrals. She raved about me (and our company) from the first big breakthrough and continued to rave.

But what *really* helped this client create her big wins?

Is it our process? The tools? The templates and sample copy?

Those are important and helpful. But if it were really about those things, it would stand to reason that every "beginner" in the field could get jaw-dropping results for all of their clients.

Of course, we all know that isn't the case.

And – of course – we deep down know that the real "secret sauce" can be found in this line:

I also want to mention your personal magic – you seem to carry a frequency around money that feels similar to my area of mastery.… It's alchemical.

We all can follow a process. What takes it to the next level, though, is who we're be-ing.

Which brings us to the Transformation Standard.

THE ART OF PERSONAL TRANSFORMATION – AS A STANDARD

Simply put, the Transformation Standard is the practice of continuous personal growth and improvement.

We can think of it as "doing the work" (oh, how we love to do the work!) full on, without bypass.

This means bettering our best, not by constant driving and striving, but because it's just something we *do*. Our continuous uplevel, into entelechy (becoming what we are becoming), just is.

I might at one time have said, it's that which is asking to be shifted by a Higher Power. And that's true, but you are the Higher Power.

These are the things that you know, deep down, are asking to be moved in order for you to get to where you want to go.

I find that the Transformation Standard is the one we talk about the least. But really, it's so important because continuous expansion requires continuous expansion, as a practice. It requires looking at the hard stuff. And doing what is required to embody the Frequency that we know is being asked of us, to create the things we say we want to create.

We're all into personal growth and development; otherwise, we wouldn't be in this business. We're always going to be engaging in personal growth work, right?

Well, yes. The Transformation Standard, however, has a few distinctions.

The first thing to know is that we're not talking about surface things. We're not talking about behavioral changes or "oh, I know it's time to stop eating carbs."

Yes, sometimes those "small" things are actually what's on the surface of the big thing!

The Transformation Standard asks us to go deep into the big thing. The big wounds, the core wounds, the deepest Shadow. And then, as time goes on, go deeper, pulling back the layers of the onion.

And meanwhile, also, the Transformation Standard is about shifting small stuff. The so-called little things. The annoyances that hang around. The stuff that you truly want to shift, and have tried to clean up, but for whatever reason, they're still in your life, and you're still not happy about it.

The Transformation Standard is about really shifting these things. Making a sacred commitment to yourself and then following through. Taking them to the "end of the line" – to whatever level is required for whatever you're creating in the moment.

And then showing up fully in the next level version of you.

And that's what distinguishes the Transformation Standard from just "working on yourself."

Everyone in this industry goes to "work on themselves." Indeed, I think a lot of people come into this industry because they love the "feeling good" part of working on themselves. But then they keep on engaging in the same behaviors.

When we manifest, we have to *let go* to let in. We must sacrifice something of a Higher Nature for a Lower Nature.

The Transformation Standard invites us to not ignore these things but look them in the eye and, when we are ready, shift them. And when we are not ready, to be fully aware that they are there and be in rapport with them.

"YOU'RE EITHER GROWING OR DYING; THERE IS NO 'STAYING THE SAME'"

There's an old saying in the personal growth world: "You're either growing or dying, but there is no 'staying the same.'"

On the one hand, I find it to be absolutely accurate. On the other hand, we can balance that with not kicking our own butts or being in constant drive-strive mode.

The Law of Vibration tells us that everything moves, nothing rests. Energy is constantly changing and shifting.

Our choice? Work with that in the highest and purest fashion, n ot for "turning ourselves into a project" (the shadow side of the Transformation Standard), but for the highest and best good.

We don't need to drive and strive. The Transformation Standard invites us to ever evolve.

When we keep expanding into our Divine Nature, we can show up fully in our Divine Nature and create what we are choosing with ease and speed.

HOW FAR ARE YOU WILLING TO GO?

How far are you willing to go? Your approach to your own growth and transformation will tell you.

The Law dictates that the Field – Creative Substance, Creative Life Force Energy, and so on. – operates completely deductively. It can't give us back anything other than what we put in. It's limited by our frequency.

Similarly – and we all know this – we can only take our clients as far as we ourselves are willing to go.

Does this mean that we have to be "ahead" of our clients? Absolutely not!

It does mean that we need to be congruent with regard to what we ask of them. Are we willing to engage in the tough stuff? Are we willing to take on the deep work, or are we just asking them to?

Not to mention the fact that holding yourself to a high standard of personal growth will give you epic superpowers with regard to the space you hold.

When you're truly going all in on your own Transformation, you can hold your clients to the standards much easier. When you go outside of YOUR comfort zone on the regular, you can ask them to go outside of theirs and be 100 percent congruent in doing so.

When you have moved some big level shit and really held yourself to that, you have so much less willingness to let people sit in their stuff.

Years ago, when I was healing my marriage, I was literally in a state of extreme "fight or flight" every day. Why? Because an old core wound had led to a massively dysregulated nervous system. By the time we got to the breaking point, the mere presence of my husband could set it off.

It was tough. I wanted to run away. But I didn't. I sat through the NLP and the therapy and the dysregulation and healed.

Guess what happens when I notice that our folks are having a hard time "going there"? Lots of patience. And ultimately, I hold the space for them to go there.

The more we hold the Transformation Standard, the easier we can hold space for others' transformation – and the next level of our own.

WHAT THE TRANSFORMATION STANDARD IS NOT

The Transformation Standard is not turning yourself into a project. It's not about always finding something within yourself that needs healing.

Sometimes you're not being asked to do the deep dive. Sometimes you're asked to take the fruits of what you've already done to the world.

We can keep healing ourselves, or we can get out there and get on with it.

The Transformation Standard is not shifting every last thing that seems to be causing you trouble. It's not about clearing every last pattern. Part of loving yourself is loving some of the things that are kind of a pain, but you've come to rely on them, and you really don't want to exert the effort to do it differently.

For example, I have what we in NLP call "a short timeline." My inner timeline is now or five minutes from now.

In other words, I "thrive" under time pressure. That is, I can sometimes do my best work, but I'm also miserable as hell when I'm feeling the crunch. (Note: I'm feeling the crunch often.)

I could change this – that is, go to the effort of "re-wiring" myself. But why would I do that? Not everything needs to be "fixed."

The Transformation Standard is not a "time out." Years ago, I was attracting clients who loved to do the "deep dive into the inner work." Unfortunately, they usually would put things off while they were doing said "inner work."

Often, I'd hear things like, "I'm going to go away and fix this or heal this and then come back and do your program."

It doesn't work that way!

Transformation does not happen when we're sitting on the mountaintop. We integrate, and transform, when we are in it, not away from it – and that includes, sometimes, a little bit of pressure. Lean into life rather than backing away from life.

The Transformation Standard is not seeing yourself as anything less than the Divine Being you are.

On the one hand, as Leaders, we grow and change and evolve.

On the other hand, in a very real way, there is nothing to do, change, or fix.

We can hold the paradox of being whole and complete without doing anything else. Remember Ariel's words: Decide you are whole and complete, and it is done. Because it is done! There is nothing else to "do."

We are perfect and called to evolve.. And remember, so are your clients.

BE THE REAL DEAL

Most influence is instant and flies under the radar. Our subconscious minds pick up on it way before our conscious mind ever does.

True influence isn't about rah-rah marketing or how many followers you have on Instagram.

It's about being the Real Deal.

With a blink of an eye, people can tell if you're the Real Deal. Your words, images, how you "present" yourself, will only confirm or deny what your clients already subconsciously know. Which then leads to whether they will trust you or not.

Then, your actions over time reinforce how trustworthy you are to invest money with you and then whether to follow you, pay attention to you, take the coaching, and ultimately get the results.

The most effective transformational practitioners understand this. Seven-Figure Leaders understand this. They know the importance of being the Real Deal.

How do you become the Real Deal?

Transformation. Cleaning up your messes and doing the difficult spiritual plus personal work. Walking the talk. Using your own teachings. Be-ing the model for the transformation you wish to see.

And, by doing so, using all of that experience and the fruits of your transformational work to care and serve your people without holding back.

KEEPING YOUR ENERGY CLEAN

Years ago, when I was in the early phases of my entrepreneurial journey but was still starting to get some traction, I was doing a lot of coaching around money.

Putting packages together. Raising fees. Coaching my clients to ask for more and then show up to deliver on the value promised. Cleaning up money messes and getting into right relationship with money.

This, I think, is where the Transformation Standard was really born. Because I saw firsthand the importance of walking the talk, talking the walk, and embodying the Frequency required to have what we Desire, and doing it with integrity.

Somewhere along the way, one of our clients asked me, "How can you charge so much and not feel like you're manipulating someone?"

The answer to that question has a value component. Put simply, if a client receives a ten-time or even twenty-five-time return on their investment over time, with the "payout" being either time or money, well, it only makes sense to charge more. It's actually a money leak if we do not. (This is the Money Impeccability Standard.)

But there is an energetic component, too.

"I feel 100 percent confident charging more because I keep my energy clean," I said. "I go to great lengths to make sure I'm not trying to 'get,' or be greedy and ask for more than what I'm bringing, or manipulate.

"All those things we are afraid of doing, with regard to money… well, they are human, in a very real sense.

"There's an easy solution: don't do them! Come from a pure place."

Now, only you can decide what a "pure place" is for you.

For me, it means coming from my Highest Level Frequency. For me, it comes from showing up as Divine, seeing money as Divine, and our clients as the Divine Beings as they are. Making the Laws my Truth rather than falling into illusion.

Over the years, I have learned that as transformational leaders, we must strive to keep our energy clean so we can show up and serve.

TRUTH: SEVEN FIGURES IN TWO YEARS OR LESS REQUIRES GROWTH

Any big leap we Desire requires a big leap internally.

Yes, you "know" this intellectually. But where are you holding back from making it real?

When we activate the Transformation Standard, there is no "holding back."

The next level of growth is inevitable because we hold OUR transformation as Standard.

Transformation just is.

The leaps happen naturally. And our clients come right along with us.

13

THE ENERGY OF DIVINE LOVE
(THE SECRET SAUCE)

I t is the summer of 2017. It is the day before the last day of a months-long campaign, and I am spiraling.

Honestly, at that time I couldn't tell you why I was spiraling. The campaign was going well – or well enough for what it was.

What it was: a relatively low-priced course and a launch designed to enroll two hundred people, our stretch goal. We weren't even remotely close, but it wasn't "bad" per se.

"A hundred sold is okay, right?" I asked myself.

I had spent so much damned time on the campaign. The planning. The writing. The shooting of the videos. The emails. The details. I never seemed to have a project manager, and I never seemed to have enough support, so that was a problem. The only team member I had who passed for a "manager" was located in Israel and was literally sleeping while I was working and vice versa.

I was all alone in my office most of the time, beavering away in a business that outwardly was doing very well (high, high multi-six figures, close to seven; I had crossed seven for a couple of years in a row), but it was taking so much from me. And never quite seemed to generate enough.

That day, all of the launching, enrolling, facilitating, leading clients, attempting to lead a team, all the successes, all the failures, all the "doing" – all of that hit me in a wave of exhaustion.

Holy shit. Will I ever be out of this grind? Will I ever get to where I want to be? What the hell am I doing all of this for? What's the point? These are years of my life.

Exhaustion was followed by hopelessness. I could feel the sadness gathering in my stomach.

To top it off, I was feeling very shaky about what I was teaching in the course I was launching. I knew it was all true, and that I was a solid teacher, but I wasn't quite living it – yet.

This is ridiculous. I am ridiculous. Who cares. This is nuts. What am I doing?

Tears started to form and gather at my eyelids, and I could feel them clambering to escape. Even though I was alone, I squeezed my eyes shut.

In that moment, I heard Her voice.

"Remember who you are."

And with it, a wave of something else. Warmth.

Kindness that, in the immortal words of the members of Spinal Tap (yes, I'm dating myself), "went to eleven."

An image formed in my mind. I could feel Her wrapping her arms around me. And I could feel all the feelings transforming all at once. The sadness melting within me in real time.

I opened my eyes and let the tears fall. I reached for a piece of paper.

I listened and began to write what I heard, all the while the warmth of Creative Substance poured in through the top of my head.

"Remember who you are. You are a priestess of Isis. You are a part of a lineage. You have been invited to bring your unique contribution of the lineage forward. You are not – in your human words – 'crazy,' you are deeply connected. Your magic is a template for Frequency magic that will heal many. That is not important right now – what is important now is to use Frequency to heal yourself."

More followed. I wrote more until there was no more. As I wrote the words, the strength came back, and slowly but surely, the warm energy began to crowd out the sadness and helplessness, gently ushering these feelings to another space and time, as if they had served their purpose.

"Never forget," Isis whispered as I felt Her wings leave my back.

I pulled myself together and, fully resourced now,

walked down to the studio, where my husband, Leland, was working on a page from his latest graphic novel.

"Help me to never forget again, okay?" I asked.

He hugged me with his own Divine Love. "I will," he said.

I walked back upstairs and watched the sales pour in. Two days later, when the doors closed and the promotion ended... we had nearly doubled our numbers.

THE SECRET SAUCE: THE ENERGY OF LOVE

Now, obviously not every campaign we have had since then has doubled in size when Isis swoops down and throws a little love into the mix. I believe, though, that She came to me in that moment, to remind me of Divine Love. To remind me that Divine Love is the "secret sauce."

Many, many great healers and spiritual teachers have spoken about the Frequency of Love and the nature of Divine Love.

How can we describe the nature of Love? And what Love is?

I won't attempt to do so here – because some things can't really adequately be described. They *can*, however, be experienced.

Most of us – and very likely, everyone reading this book – have experienced Divine Love. Here, as we near the final chapter, my intention is to help you remember, as Isis helped me remember those years ago.

Divine Love is a Frequency. It is the Frequency of Truth. The Frequency of Divine Law. The Frequency of Connection. The Frequency of Source.

Like all things, it comes from Source and is of Source. The origination.

Throughout this book, we have been exploring the breaking free of illusion. You have been seeing the lies for what they are, and aligning with what "just is."

Now, as we come to the last Standard and last Frequency, or energy, or "switch" in this sequence… we come to the most potent "just is-ness" of them all.

Divine Love Is. Divine Love Just Is.

Indeed, Divine Love is *all* there is, and all that need be.

It is Source. It is abundance. It is the energy of Creative Substance that we have all around us. The supply is infinite. We have endless love to tap into, receive, and give.

There is infinite supply. We can never use it all up and it will never run out.

When we incarnate into our human form, we lose sight of this truth and buy into the illusion. Then we have experiences that reinforce the illusions and create more painful experiences.

None of that changes the Truth of Love.

Love just is. Divine Love is. We are Divine; therefore, we are Divine Love, and therefore, we just *are* love . There is nothing to be "done" but notice that plain and simple fact.

When we feel the Inner Friction, the negative emotions, we have thoughts or experiences that trigger very real chemical processes in our body. The circumstances are very real. There are good reasons to disconnect from Love.

Disconnection from Love is part of the human experience, but it is not Truth.

This is what Isis was really trying to tell me, all those years ago. She came to me, Divine BE-ing to Divine Be-ing, and used the energy of Love to bring me back to the Truth of Love.

Divine Love just is, and with this final Standard, we use this truth to transmute any remaining Inner Friction into the rocket fuel that blasts us forward.

WHAT WE'RE ALL SEEKING: LOVE

Being seen, accepted, and, yes, loved is the deepest need of humans. It is fundamental to our survival. So much so that our greatest primal fear is being kicked out of the tribe.

Years ago, before things like Facebook and Instagram, before cities, before malls, highways and houses, there were small communities in harsh conditions. Get kicked out of the group and into the harsh conditions, and you wouldn't survive for long.

Underneath this baseline primal survival fear is the fear that we are unlovable. We also are secretly afraid that we will run *out* of love. And so we turn ourselves inside out to "get love," which only adds to the illusion that we need to "get" it.

When children have love, they thrive. When they do not have love, they whither quickly.

The same is true for adults, it's just hidden beneath years of coping and armor and a skill set for skating through the world that has been devoid of love, or missing love, or full of abuses and injustices that are cries for love masquerading as cries for power.

What does all this mean for us?

It means, as Leaders, as those with the awareness, that we realize the power of Love is a strong power indeed. And that, as Leaders, we understand that the human experience is full of deep hurt and deep injustice. And, at the same time, we can use the power of Love to completely turn any situation around.

Love truly *is* the secret sauce.

A KEY TO LOVE: THE RADICAL ACCEPTANCE OF WHAT IS

About six months before Isis gave me my break-through, I'd had another breakthrough. This time in a seminar room in California.

I had traveled there from Portland, as I'd traveled many times before. The seminar was with NLP Marin, the lineage of NLP that I'd had extensive training in, over many such weekends, in years previous.

On Day One, our trainers, Carla and Carl, sent us out into the courtyard of the hotel.

"Find a tree, or a rock or a bench, or something that appeals to you. Then, withdraw your consent to its existence."

Just for fun because we can, I invite you to put the book down and give it a shot. Use something on your desk. A pen, perhaps.

Pick up the pen. Look at the pen.

Then, take back your consent to the pen's existence.

Even if you're just imagining it (come on, you did put the book down, didn't you?), you may notice that this is truly a tricky endeavor.

And yet... if you think about it, we are doing this *all the time*.

(This was the point of the exercise, to make us

aware of how much we do this, which is to say, *all the time*.)

How do we withdraw consent?

- Feeling hurt by the client who backed out of our program after they had a huge breakthrough with your help. Taking it personally (because, you know, it kind of is personal).
- Feeling frustrated that clients aren't getting bigger results, faster. Feeling frustrated with yourself that you can't seem to help them "make it happen."
- Feeling sad and angry at a team member who left you high and dry on the eve of a big campaign.
- Feeling fed up and frustrated that you spent two to three months marketing a program and only getting a third of the enrollments you wanted.
- Being so angry when right after you manifested that $100k client, you (just as quickly) manifested a healing crisis that put you on bed rest for two weeks.

What is resistance and letting Inner Friction run the show but withdrawing consent to a situation that already *just is*? (Yes, the situations we *don't* want "just are," too!)

This is resistance to the present state.

What does resistance to the present state do? Robs us of choice.

When we're fighting, when we're battling – with the situation, with fatigue, with the client who did XYZ – we create even more difficulty to make the changes we want to make.

We stay stuck.

And we know this, right? All of the energy that we could be investing in change is going into resisting.

The truth that we resist the most is that resistance is in the mind and is a choice.

But there are other choices. When we consent to what *is*, we release the resistance, and instantly more choices find themselves on the table.

We regain connection.

We have access to Divine Love, which already is, and is infinite. We have access to power.

USING DIVINE LOVE TO INSTANTLY MELT RESISTANCE

For a quick example of how quickly Divine Love can change things around, try this…

Think of something that you have wanted to change for a long time but hasn't changed.

Maybe it's weight loss. Maybe it's debt. Maybe it's that you've been trying for *so long* to call in your life partner and yet you continue to spend Christmases alone.

Now, really think about it. Really take in the situation. This is something that hasn't changed. In *so* long!! You've been stuck with it. Carrying it around like a ball and chain. You've tried to get rid of it before and failed. Probably, it's like failure after failure.

Go ahead and dial up that feeling. *Really* lean into it. Really notice that you're resisting this present state. It sucks. You hate it. Yet here it is, sticking to you like the strongest, stickiest glue, snaring everything you touch with the stickiness into more stickiness.

Notice how terrible this really is. The magnitude of the situation. I mean, you've lost *years* of your life to this. Literally. Let's not sugarcoat.

Allow yourself to feel *that*. Keep going until you can no longer stand it.

And then …. Take a deep breath, and allow yourself to shrug and go….

OK.

It is what it is.

It just is.

Notice yourself relax. And from this place, notice that there is a portal to a stream of pure Divine Love, floating about three inches out in front of your forehead.

Allow the Divine Love from the stream to flow in

through the top of your head, down through your head, through your neck and shoulders, down your arms.

This is the energy of Divine Love here, so really allow yourself to receive Divine Love. Feel Love. Feel the love pouring all over you, through you, and notice that hey, this feels familiar. Because when you have activated your Highest Self, you feel this feeling.

Allow love to strengthen you. Feel that strength grow.

Meanwhile, allow yourself to notice that the Divine Love "tap" is still flowing. It shows no signs of stopping. You sense the Love flowing out of your feet now, and it is pooling up around your ankles in the most delightful way.

Now , from *this* place...

What would you like to create in your life?

IMPORTANT SIDE NOTE: FULL AWARENESS OF WHAT IS

If we're talking about Consenting to the Shitty Things That Are, or our own resistance, or the resistance of clients, or the resistance Brian (the brain) inevitably puts up to the co-creation of our businesses to take them from six to seven figures, then it's important to understand what we are NOT doing.

Because one of the reasons why people stay stuck

in resistance is because they confuse "Okay" (acceptance) with "It's okay" (apathy or indifference).

We are surrounded by circumstances and situations that are simply *not* okay.

What's more, each and every one of us has had the kinds of experiences here in "Earth School" that take us years to get over. Abuse, loss, and so on.

These things are *not* okay.

Sometimes, things are just *not* okay.

And yet – like Divine Love, like your Divine nature – they just *are*. They may not be okay. But here they are.

Withdrawing our consent sets us up in a dangerous place of holding on to them while, at the same time, in a very real way denying our reality.

Years ago, a mentor said to me, "What you can't be with owns you."

We don't want to deny reality, obviously. But when we withdraw our consent to things that currently *are*, they own us.

LEAN INTO CONFLICT: POUR ON LOVE

Another part of the radical acceptance that gives us access to Love is to lean *in* rather than lean *out*.

How often do we get the email, the credit card bounces, the team member quits at the end of a launch or the beginning of a launch, and we lean out?

We ignore the email, ignore the texts, curl up

with Netflix and the closest thing to artisan ice cream that we can find at the grocery store rather than confronting the launch situation head on.

I don't need to tell you what kinds of delays and messes this creates!

Instead, consent fully. Get your choice back. Pour on love.

DIVINE LOVE IS THE MULTIPLIER

When our clients find their way to us, they are struggling with big challenges in their business. They feel the struggle of "the slog" – feeling like they're working their butts off to launch, have all the sales calls, call in the clients, grow the business, manage the team, and more.

They *all* say some form of:

"I want things to be easier. I want to collapse time."

What they are really saying is:

"I'm ready for more."

More clients, free time, time with their kids, time for other things in their life, more results, the second business (because what do so many ambitious women do when they get one business running smoothly without them? They start another…), and – of course – more money.

And isn't that what you Desire, too, my dear reader?

You want more money because *more* is a Desire of your heart as well as being a reflection of all the effort you are putting in and the dreams you have.

What you may not know in those sloggy moments is that there *is* more.

There is more, and it's here right now.

There is infinite supply. While they may experience lack in their life (lack of time, money, resources, etc.), the Truth is abundance just is.

While there is always some doing to bring those outward expressions of *"more"* to the physical, 3D plane… *more* is already here.

The energy of Divine Love is more. And we don't have to "do" anything to receive it.

It costs nothing to give it, and nothing to receive it. We can give it and receive it at will.

Will you?

14

THE POWER OF SURRENDER

"*The brain can't believe it's this easy. But it is.*"

Over the years, since Ariel answered my question – is instant transformation even possible? – I keep coming back to this fact.

The truth is scaling your business to seven figures as an experienced coach, healer, or teacher isn't easy. It's simple, but it's not easy.

Except that... perhaps underneath it all, it is. After all, what is business but connecting our gift – be it a physical product, a service, a modality, a skill, a transformation – to someone who can use it most, and then through our delivery, empowering them to do just that?

At the end of the day, this is essentially what a business does.

So why *not* allow it to be easy?

"Simple but not easy" is an adage that bears out.

It can be easy. But it is *not* easy – not because it is un-simple, or un-easy, but because of the simple things that happen within the business and our brain's stories about them.

I believe that seven figures as a coach, healer, or teacher is a worthy goal. I believe that we need more Leaders who have taken upon themselves the challenge of leading.

We have a *lot* within us that is set up to make us stop – to give in when things get hard or to have things take a long time.

The problem is when we stop, when we give in to "hard," we give up our dreams. For conscious experts and transformational leaders, it's about not just dreams but our mission and service to our clients as well.

I believe that Isis and the Creative Team (my name for what you can think of as spirit guides) gave me the Standards to make things easier.

But as a Leader, it's up to you, and nobody else, to navigate the natural challenges that turns something as simple as "have a gift, find a person to give it to, deliver service, repeat" into a hard slog and drain on the nervous system.

If you're at the end of this book, you are already a Leader. I honor you for all that you have done (and all hands seen and unseen) that have brought you to this point.

And today, in this moment, like every day and

every moment, you are at a choice point.

You can choose a smoother path. You can choose to have your experience of business be easier. You can choose to make leaps instead of incremental steps.

You can choose to collapse time.

It requires, however, that you choose to surrender. To release the resistance and Inner Friction that make your day-to-day experience feel hard, so you can embody higher levels of Frequency that naturally call forward the opportunities to have the business that you want.

The Inner Friction that we've been talking about comes from pushing against the "bad" parts of running our business that *just are*. The more we push and resist that which Just Is and the more we buy into stories and illusions about whatever is going on in a given day, the "harder" our experience becomes.

The Standards were given to me to help you surrender the struggle and instead align with Truth : the Truth about you and the spiritual Truths that, when we use them in an empowered way, can help us to create miracles.

It's up to *you* to use them, though.

The Standards are a tool of conscious awareness. Keep them front and center and act from them in the moment.

Here are just a few challenges that will continue to slow you down, without a clear choice to surrender your resistance around them, and without empowering tools to move through them when they show up in the day-to-day.

CHALLENGE #1: ADDICTED TO STRUGGLE

We say we want things to be easier, but *do we?*

You wouldn't always think so, given how many Leaders fall into making things harder on themselves than they need to be!

Ah, but then again, we all have a certain "addiction" to struggle – our brain sets it up that way! Our "critter brain," or reptilian brain, wants to maintain the status quo of "not dead" and will set it up so that we do all the things we've done before, even if they are fundamentally damaging, to ensure that we stay "not dead."

This leads to a commitment to struggle that can feel like an addiction. Remember, the critter brain's criterion for useful patterns is "did I survive this before," where survival equals "not dead"!

So it will keep bringing us back to "struggle" over and over and over again.

To the brain, what we see as states of "struggle" are really survival patterns that were set up early in life – patterns that we will repeat, over and over again, if we don't have a way to deal with them, especially in the moment.

CHALLENGE #2: CONSTANT ILLUSIONS (A.K.A. FLAT-OUT *LIES*)

"Don't believe a word I say," says master trainer and entrepreneur T. Harv Eker. "And don't believe a thought you think."

The brain creates illusions. Actually, the brain creates blatant *lies*!

If we do not have a reliable way of spotting illusion lies and busting them continually or moving forward in spite of them, we will allow what we see in front of us to become our Truth.

You're conditioned to believe what your eyes and physical senses tell you. It takes continual, sustained effort to shift that. It will not happen on its own.

Frequency helps us with both the spotting of illusion lies and the busting of them.

CHALLENGE #3: OUR ENVIRONMENT

The people and things we choose to have around us are some of the strongest sources of influence in our lives. We will actually bring our own energy up or down to match the energy of the people and spaces around us.

We get constant validation from our environment, and it shapes us, which means that conscious leaders must be intentional about their environment.

Sometimes, though, we can't shift our environment. So we get to demand that those in our world calibrate to US by holding a high Frequency.

The "trick," of course, is holding it ourselves.

CHALLENGE #4: UNCONSCIOUS AGREEMENTS WITH OTHER PEOPLE

Human beings have two sources of "survival patterns."

The first is when our physical safety is threatened. Physical trauma. Feeling like we're not on solid physical ground. When our physical safety is threatened , we do not meet the requirements of the bottom of Maslow's Hierarchy of Needs pyramid.

Makes sense, and most of us can easily relate to and understand this. The other, however, is a lot more sneaky and subtle, and that is the groups we're a part of. Because our lineage dictates that "being kicked out of the tribe" is Enemy #1, our #1 Primal Fear, we humans create unconscious (and conscious) agreements and loyalties to the groups we're a part of. Family groups – your agreement to your mother that you will never "outshine" her, for example – friends, communities.

The pain, inner conflict, and deeply shitty money beliefs held by spiritual communities are a good example of this. Years ago, those in power installed the belief of "money is bad" in spiritual people to keep them down. The belief is long, LONG outdated and untrue, and yet it continues to rule the lives of many people, including transformational leaders.

If we are to effectively lead, we must release the unconscious agreements and loyalties with groups we're a part of.

CHALLENGE #5: FROM INFO TO EMBODIMENT

We can learn "all the things" but until it's embodied, it's just information.

Or, as one of my old teachers used to put it, "Information is just a rumor until it's in the body."

The art of Seven-Figure Transformational Leadership – and using it to grow a seven-figure business – is no different. Just as we can collect "all the strategies" and tactics to get clients, make money, and scale, if we're not using them, all of it is "just a rumor." And we can learn the foolproof path to collapsing time to seven-figures, but if we are not embodied in our Leadership, we will be at a disadvantage.

The Standards are no different. The Standards are incredibly powerful – some of the most powerful frequency work I have ever experienced. I have seen massive, massive transformation in our clients who really take them on and embody them.

Without practice and embodiment, though, they are just more info.

Info must move to awareness, then breakthrough, then continued practice and experience until we own it. The same is true of your Seven-Figure Leadership.

WE'RE BEING ASKED

The challenges I name here are real challenges. Real obstacles. They affect you pretty much every day, whether you are conscious of them or not. Looking at them square in the eyes can be really difficult because, deep down, we know that doing so presents us with an invitation.

We know, on some level, that as Seven-Figure Leaders, we're being *asked to do exactly that*.

We are asked to say *yes* to what we know is possible. Asked to say *yes* to what (deep down) we know is already here. Asked to get out of "victim mode" for good – no matter how high-performing or successful we are. Asked to say *yes* to our full-on Creative Power.

I believe that the high-performing, experienced coaches, healers, conscious experts, spiritual teachers, and consultants are being called forward at this time.

Those of us who have dived down deep into how humans change, how we break free, are being called.

Because the collective consciousness continues to awaken. Time continues to speed up.

We need Leaders who can guide us on the next evolution of our journey and do it while modeling things like what it means to have money, what it means to receive lots of money for one's work, and doing it in a way that creates a great lifestyle.

Not to mention, your dreams. Your dreams are important. But they will not happen without one key move by you, which is to surrender to what is being asked (by Spirit, your purpose, yourself) instead of continuing to hold on to the Inner Friction and resistance that keeps them from coming in.

THE ART OF SURRENDER

"Surrender" can mean many things. In this case – your acceptance of the invitation to Seven-Figure Leadership – surrender is the release of resistance and the saying of *yes* to all of our good, our purpose, what we are meant to manifest and contribute in this lifetime.

Our surrendering to what is being asked of us to create what we want, and the surrendering of the resistance that keeps us from getting it, is the activation of Creative Power.

The Standards are the art of surrender in action.

The Standards can be part of *your* solution.

When we shift our Frequency into that of a Seven-Figure Leader, we can see the opportunities and take action on them. But we can't do it alone.

It takes commitment and practice and a willingness to stay the course until the shift becomes automatic.

You are the new paradigm. When you step into a fully embodied Seven-Figure Frequency, you give everyone around you permission to do the same. It's a massive ripple effect.

Will you say yes to what is being asked, to create what you want?

Will you allow it to feel easier and be easier?

15

YOUR SEVEN-FIGURE BUSINESS
IS HERE NOW

M ay 2004. I am sitting at the gate at the Barcelona airport, about to make the most important decision of my life.

Next to me is the man I had been dating for the past two years. We were here for a comics convention, where he was the guest of honor.

Our relationship is at a turning point. We have talked about marriage. I *wanted* to get married. And it was time to decide. We lived on opposite sides of the country, and for the past two years, we had been flying back and forth to see each other at regular intervals.

That boyfriend was, and is, an amazing human. Caring. Considerate. Loving. Devoted. And very, very well known in the comics industry (still is). Our two years together had been solid.

Problem was, there was another man. Also on the

opposite side of the country. He and I had only seen each other in person once – if you could call our meeting at a comics show in San Francisco a "meeting," since he had barely taken his eyes off his drawing when I stopped by his table. His head hidden under the brim of a baseball cap, he glanced up once, smiled, and nodded and then buried his face again as the young man next to me leaned over and said, "This guy's stuff is the best in the entire show."

Nonetheless, I had managed to slip the baseball-cap guy a couple of zines I had made about my adventures playing Irish fiddle on the New York City subway – my first attempt at writing something real, an act I had hoped would give me the confidence to make more things and, ultimately, to convince someone like Mr. "Best In Show" to partner with me on a comics project.

Six months later, Leland sent me a letter, having found the zines in a box of stuff from the show. "These are really good," he said, and in short order, we were communicating ten times per day.

"She has a boyfriend," he told his good friend Maria.

"She has two," Maria replied.

Leland was *also* in a relationship. Marriage had also been on the table.

Most of the Barcelona trip had been spent talking to Leland. What with my boyfriend doing "guest of honor" stuff, I had been left to roam the cobblestone streets and cute little cafes on my own. I spent most of it pining.

The night before, while lying in bed, the boyfriend had asked me if I had feelings for Leland. "I think so," I answered honestly.

And now, sitting at our gate, waiting for our flight back to LA, the boyfriend was on my left side, and I was trying to keep it together while I was, well, pondering what might possibly be the most important decision of my life.

I didn't have to ponder long. Indeed, I didn't have to ponder at all, because my knowing was instant. Channels open, I consulted the Old Gods.

The boyfriend was not the guy.

The decision was made before I boarded the plane. I broke the news when we touched down on the other side of the country.

The sweet boyfriend begged me to stay. Kind of. For a few minutes. But he knew, too.

Relationship done, new life to come. Two weeks later, Leland was in New York. Two days after that, we decided to get married.

Decision made, I stepped from one reality into another.

I had collapsed time.

THE MOST IMPORTANT THING YOU CAN TAKE AWAY FROM THIS BOOK

The key takeaway from this book is the understanding that everything you well and truly Desire is already here.

Whatever you want – such as, for instance, a seven-figure transformational business – is here now. You can have it. The only "waiting" is the waiting to take it from the multidimensional realms to the 3D.

The only "waiting" is for the body to catch up, as it were.

One of our "un-rules" at 7-Figure Goddess® is that you get to have it how you want it. If you want to make a certain amount of money, you can do it. If you want to offer a particular transformation, you can do it. If you want your business to give you twenty hours off per week, you can do it.

If you want an easy- peasy, low overhead, low stress seven-figures from your Highest Level Work as you spend most of your "in the biz" time actually working with clients and creating transformation, you can do that.

The only catch is, you must claim it now. And then embody the version of you – the Frequency – of the one who already has it.

If you want a seven-figure transformational biz, then you must show up as the seven-figure transformational leader you already are, here, in the 3D.

The thoughts. The actions. The energy signature. Fully embodied, for real, as much of the time as possible.

The Standards invite us to relax into Truths that just are, Truths that support us rather than engage and indulge the lies that keep us in a state of tension, keep us in a state of internal dysregulation, keep us questioning ourselves and holding back.

The Standards are an easier way to live and a way, *way* easier way to run your business.

But we must say *yes* to fully activating and embodying them.

And we must do it now. There is no time but now.

Soooo many super-smart, highly intelligent, high-performing women, especially those who know personal development and have read Ekhart Tolle seven times, are still disconnected from the now.

They are still one-foot-in, one-foot-out.

Many years ago, when I was still in my twenties and was still blissfully unaware of how I habitually used avoidance as a trauma response and coping mechanism, I had a mantra.

"This is fine for now."

Sure, I'll date this guy – it's fine for now.

Sure, I'll take this job – fine for now.

I like computer science well enough. I need to go to grad school, so I'll just do this for now.

I'm fine for now with the weight I'm at.

This debt? It's not much. It's fine for now.

Some of this exploration was positive. And leading me in the right direction. (Okay, sure, all of this, it could be argued, was leading me in the right direction.)

The problem with "fine for now," though, is that it hides the key energy it represents and activates: *later*.

In our early twenties, we don't fully understand "later." We don't understand how dangerous "later" really is.

And if we're not careful, we can continue to buy into that illusion.

Looking back, I didn't need to spend all that time finding myself – when really, I was just afraid. I had been conditioned to be afraid, to put myself in the role of the Bad Girl, "bad and wrong" because I wasn't following my family's wishes... "bad and wrong" because I chose magic.

Chose, I did... but I didn't really throw myself into the deep end.

That was for "later."

Of course, intellectually, we know the truth. The facts.

"Later" is a total fantasy. "Later" may never get here.

The only time is *now*.

One of my teachers likes to ask a confronting question. Are you looking for a way out, or are you looking for a way IN?

If you are really, truly looking for a way to collapse time on your goals, to grow a sustainable seven-figure business that actually nourishes you, that gives you wings, that expresses your purpose and multiplies your impact, it's not going to "just happen."

You must Decide. And the way appears.

Your Seven-Figure Frequency is the way in. The Standards is a simple way to slide into that Frequency and stay there.

I would love to help you do just that.

Until then, keep leading…

ACKNOWLEDGMENTS

The birth of the Standards (and therefore this book) came in early 2018, when I was struggling with an automated webinar funnel, of all things.

If you don't know what an automated webinar funnel is, no worries – all you need to know is that I *didn't* want to be working on one. I *didn't* want to spend all my time trying to sell an online course on manifesting, either. I *thought* I wanted to be a creator of a manifesting course while on my way to being "the next Gabby Bernstein," manifesting teacher to the stars.

But as it turns out, I *didn't* want that – yet. I wanted to coach. I wanted to teach transformational leaders how to make more money than most doctors. I wanted to figure out what I really had to say about manifesting, magic, metaphysics, collapsing time, making money, creating your own reality, and marketing (which is really just another magical tool).

One of my clients-turned-friends at the time, Amira Alvarez, saw that too. And with just a few words, she helped me see my next step. Within minutes of that conversation, I pushed everything else aside and spent ten days at the kitchen table, channeling what was to become my next body of work in the online business coaching realm, and the Standards.

Thank you, Amira. I am, as you might say, ever grateful.

The next wave of gratitude goes to our clients, whose deep love of the Standards and radical results from using them let me know that I was really onto something. Big thanks especially to the first few cohorts of Highest Level Transformation (the program that the Standards were created for) and our biggest "Standards Supporters," including my dear friends Penelope Jane Smith, Joy Bufalini, Marcelle della Faille and the glorious Kim Coles. Big thanks to the members of the Highest Level Leader Collective (who use the Standards every day) and also to the members of the first round of the companion course that goes with this book.

Of course, I must give all the gratitude to my teachers and partners in magic and Universal Law. This list is long – for the full scoop, check out the "Lineage" page on our website at www.7FigureGod dess.com. Extra special big thanks to David Neagle, who I consider to be *the* greatest living teacher of the Laws working today, and his CEO, Steph Tuss. Thanks to Jennifer Longmore, founder of Soul Journeys®, from whom I have learned so much magic. And to my Protean family, and the

Entelechy girls – my magic was truly birthed with you.

This book was written during a period of big transition at 7-Figure Goddess®. I am so, *so* grateful for our extraordinary team: MaryAnn McNulty, Kailey Abbruzzi, Kristina Shands, my dear friend Jessica Daniels (who has taken every business photo of me since 2013, including the photos used in this book), and Halle Eavelyn. Thanks, too, to Tamika Auwai, whose presence is still felt (and whose content we still use!) so many years later – as always, I am grateful for our continued connection, Goddess, and your influence on the Standards. Thanks to all the fine folks at NLP Marin, whose teachings have influenced Feminine Magic® greatly over the years. Thank you to Travis Sago, my brother-in-offers and fellow "matchmaker" – the depth of your contribution to my work and world cannot be overstated. And to the Mojo Mastermind, for bearing witness to so much growth over the years.

Special shout-out to my magical sister Danielle Rama Hoffman and Thoth, Isis, and the Divine and Creative Teams for giving me the loving reflection (read: kick in the pants!) on that day in July 2022 that *finally* had me saying *yes* to writing this book. Of course, Isis, Thoth, Joan, the Record Keepers, and the Creative Team always have my thanks and love for being my constant companions on the journey, and my direct line to Source Consciousness.

Big thanks to Halle, Kim, and Rachel Headley – a.k.a. the Queen Posse – for all their love and support, and the Egyptian Queens. Our coming together for the trip of a lifetime was no coincidence. Thank you, Julie Eason, for always holding the vision. Thank you to Linda Bard for being such an amazing friend.

Thanks always, *always* go to my two greatest loves and all-time favorite persons: Leland and Brigit Purvis. You inspire me, keep me going, and bring so much joy to my daily world. It is truly a blessing to do life with you. I love you. To my family: Mom, Dad, Mike, Angie, Lisa, Mark, Joey, Taylor, and Seb – you always have my love.

Finally, thank you to all the women and men of the 7-Figure Goddess® community: those who came before, those who are Here Now, and those who will be here soon. Thanks to *you*, dear reader, for daring Desire such a thing as a seven-figure transformational business! Thank *you* for mastery, commitment, and showing up every day. Thank *you* for your role in the evolution of consciousness on the planet.

ABOUT THE AUTHOR

Elizabeth Purvis is the premier offers and messaging strategist for high-performing transformational leaders ready to scale to seven figures and beyond.

She is the founder and CEO of 7-Figure Goddess®, where her specialty is leading experienced coaches, healers, mentors, and spiritual teachers to embody their Highest Level and scale their businesses without webinars, launches, or sales calls.

One of the first teachers of the "big ticket" model of packaging transformational services, Elizabeth combines over fifteen years of expertise in offers, messaging, and online marketing strategy with two decades of metaphysical practice to empower her clients to manifest their money goals while delivering their soul-purpose work. Her clients' phenomenal, real-world results are known and unparalleled in the industry.

Elizabeth holds a master's degree in computer science from New York University, certification in the Transformational Coaching Method (The Health Coach Institute), and a master's level certification in neuro-linguistic programming from NLP Marin. She is a proud Wiccan initiate (Protean Tradition) and certified Akashic Records teacher (Souljourneys.ca). She spent ten years as a systems engineer in Silicon Alley and did a stint in the comics industry before leaving both to honor her calling to "be a part of the movement to bring magic to the mainstream."

A priestess and practitioner of Western esoteric traditions for over twenty years, Elizabeth is also the creator of Feminine Magic®, a set of practices for women to develop their co-creative power. Raised in Maine and schooled in New York City, Elizabeth now lives in Portland, Oregon, in "a cute little four-story farmhouse" with her husband, the artist Leland Purvis, and their daughter, Brigit.

Elizabeth and her team are on a mission to help coaches, healers, and conscious experts create high multi-six- and seven-figure businesses. Discover more of her work and the 7-Figure Goddess® community at 7FigureGoddess.com.

THANK YOU FOR READING

Thank you for reading this book! More importantly, thank you for accepting the Divine assignment that is being in business as a transformational leader.

Our mission at 7-Figure Goddess® is to bring consciousness-raising work (magic) to the mainstream by helping 1000+ coaches, healers, conscious experts, teachers scale to high multi-six or seven figures – without being dependent on things like webinars, automated funnels, big launches, or sales calls.

If you're ready to make the leap from six figures to seven, and you're ready for your Frequency (who you be) to do some of the heavy lifting as described in this book, we have some gifts for you.

Head on over to www.7FigureGoddess Book.com to claim the gifts that go with this book. You'll find a free companion class, a printable

PDF cheat sheet with the Standards that you can keep by your desk, inspiring stories from our clients, and quite possibly a surprise or two!

We also have a companion course that goes with this book – a potent program where I'll walk you through "switching on" your Highest Level Frequency using the Standards. The course is where you'll *embody* each of the Standards, so you can go from your current income level to $50k-$100k months and beyond with more ease and speed. You'll learn all about it and have the opportunity to join when you watch the free class at www.7FigureGod dessBook.com.

Then, be sure to connect with us online in all the places:

Website: www.7FigureGoddess.com
Facebook: www.facebook.com/7FigureGoddess
My personal Facebook: www.facebook.com/elizpurvis
Instagram: www.instagram.com/elizpurvis/
LinkedIn: www.linkedin.com/in/elizabethpurvis/
I'd love to hear what "ahas" dropped in for you as you read this book. You can email me at eliz abeth@7figuregoddess.com.